GW00818592

the OFFICE

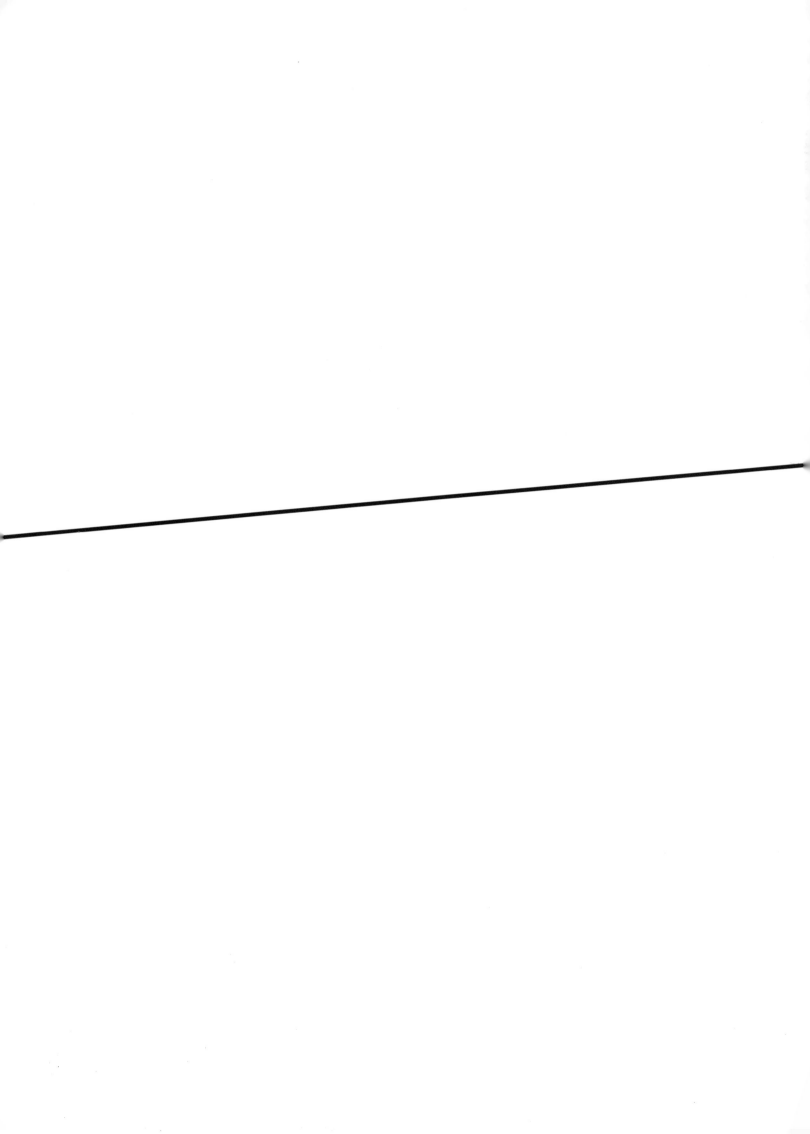

DESIGNING FOR SUCCESS

the OFFICE

STEPHEN CRAFTI

Published in Australia in 2004 by
The Images Publishing Group Pty Ltd
ABN 89 059 734 431
6 Bastow Place, Mulgrave, Victoria, 3170, Australia
Telephone: +61 3 9561 5544 Facsimile: +61 3 9561 4860
Email: books@images.com.au
Website: www.imagespublishinggroup.com

Copyright © The Images Publishing Group Pty Ltd 2004
The Images Publishing Group Reference Number: 554

National Library of Australia
Cataloguing-in-Publication entry:

Crafti, Stephen, 1959– .

Designing for success: the office.

ISBN 1 920744 65 7.

1. Office buildings – Design and construction – Pictorial works.
2. Office layout – Pictorial works.
3. Interior architecture – Pictorial works. I. Title.

725.23

Designed by The Graphic Image Studio Pty Ltd, Mulgrave, Australia
Website: www.tgis.com.au

Film by Mission Productions Limited
Printed by Max Production Printing & Book-binding Limited

IMAGES has included on its website a page for special notices in relation to this and our other publications.
Please visit this site: www.imagespublishinggroup.com

CONTENTS

INTRODUCTION
Stephen Crafti   7

CURVES
Architektonic   8

ON THE EDGE
H2O   12

THE FEEL OF A CAMPUS
Geyer   18

INTO A NEW MILLENNIUM
Williams Boag Pty Ltd Architects   22

A NEW FRONTIER
Architektonic   28

A LONG RECTILINEAR SPACE
Baenziger Coles   34

THE RIGHT MESSAGE
Gray Puksand   36

A WINTER ROOM
Carr Design   40

HOME AND OFFICE
Carr Design   44

A SMALL GEM
Neil + Idle Architects   46

CREATING A STORM
Bligh Voller Nield   50

AS OPEN AS IT GETS
Bligh Voller Nield   56

AHEAD OF ITS TIME
Denton Corker Marshall Architects   60

SENSE OF DISCOVERY
Woods Bagot   62

A DESIGN CLASSIC
Bates Smart   64

AN EYE FOR DETAIL
Jan Manton Architects   70

A 1970S CLASSIC
John Kenny Architect   74

A JOURNEY
Stephen Jolson Architect Pty Ltd   76

STUDIO STYLE
McBride Charles Ryan – Architecture + Interior Design   80

PROGRESSIVE
BBP Architects   86

WORKING FROM HOME
Form Architecture Furniture   90

GRAPHIC
Melocco and Moore Architects   96

CREATING A DIVISION
Doyle Architect Pty Ltd   100

ONCE A FACTORY
Craig Rossetti Architect   104

DOWN A LANE
Bird de la Coeur Architects   110

BLURRING THE LINES
Architects Johannsen + Associates Pty Ltd   116

TRANSPARENT
Jackson Clements Burrows Architects   122

JUST LANDED
Minifie Nixon   126

WELL CONNECTED
Inarc Architecture   132

THE ENERGY AT LUXE
Neometro Architects   136

VICTORIAN HOTEL
Grant Amon Architects Pty Ltd   140

FROM THE INSIDE OUT
Harmer Architecture Pty Ltd   142

DARE TO BE DIFFERENT
Six Degrees   146

THE RIGHT SERVICE
Multiplicity   148

THE RIGHT IMAGINATION
Anne Crampton Architect   152

CENTRE OF TOWN
Stanic Harding Architects   156

OVER THIRTEEN FLOORS
Peckvonhartel   162

SUBSTANCE
Hassell   164

A COMPLETE MAKEOVER
Hassell   170

A VICTORIAN SHOPFRONT
David Neil Architects   174

NEW LIFE FOR AN EIGHTIES BUILDING
SJB Architects   178

DESIGNED FOR A LIFETIME
Whittaker Hadenham Openshaw Pty Ltd   184

A SENSE OF THE PAST
Whittaker Hadenham Openshaw Pty Ltd   190

OVER SIX LEVELS
Whittaker Hadenham Openshaw Pty Ltd   196

INSPIRATIONAL
Di Donato   202

RESPONDING TO THE SITE
Lyons   204

TWO IN ONE
Shelton Finnis Pty Ltd   208

A LEAFY ENCLAVE
Bruce Marshall Architects   212

GOING TO WORK
Coy & Yiontis Pty Ltd   214

ONE LARGE SPACE
Cassandra Fahey   220

SYMMETRICAL
Guilford Bell + Graham Fisher Architects   222

Acknowledgments   224

Index of Architects   224

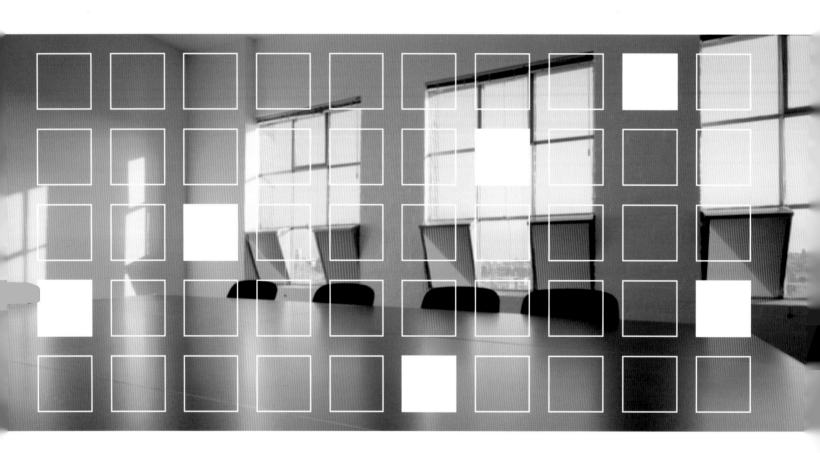

INTRODUCTION

STEPHEN CRAFTI

LIKE WORKING HOURS, WHICH HAVE CHANGED SIGNIFICANTLY OVER THE YEARS, SO TOO HAVE THE PLACES WE WORK IN. OFFICES, ONCE ENCLOSED TO ENSURE PRIVACY, ARE IN MANY CASES, OPEN AND TRANSPARENT. THERE ARE FEW DIVIDING SCREENS AND LARGE BENCHES OR TABLES SERVICE A NUMBER OF STAFF. INSTEAD OF HARD PLASTER WALLS TO DEFINE SEPARATE OFFICES AND MEETING ROOMS, TRANSLUCENT GLASS IS USED. HOWEVER, WHILE THE MAJORITY OF OFFICES, BOTH COMMERCIAL AND DOMESTIC, ARE NOW 'OPEN PLAN', MANY STILL INCLUDE PRIVATE SPACES WHERE CLIENTS WILL NOT BE OVERHEARD. THE DIRECTOR OF A COMPANY MAY HAVE HIS OR HER OWN OFFICE, BUT THIS OFFICE IS READILY ACCESSIBLE TO ALL STAFF.

Finishes and materials used in the home now appear in offices. Textured wallpaper, which adds a sense of warmth to a home, is also used in a boardroom to create a more intimate atmosphere. Likewise, colour is often generously applied to walls or provided by art and furniture. While the corporate black leather armchair is still a favourite, there are numerous alternatives. In one office for example, beanbags are scattered. In another office, 'exercise balls' provide staff with another option for how they want to work.

Perforated mesh screens conceal services or double as pin boards for staff to display work. And recycled materials add a unique feel to some offices. For example, a steel mesh curtain, once used as a conveyor belt to process food, now acts as a veil to a meeting room.

The offices illustrated in this book are diverse. However, there are common themes, one being comfort and the ability for staff to relax and move around the space. In one office, several tables are simply joined together without any partitions. There was concern that no staff member should sit at the one table for too long. As a result staff are encouraged to change seats regularly, providing fresh stimulation.

This book highlights some of the changes that have occurred in office design over recent years. Whether the office is large in scale or simply a small area at home, the spaces are designed to suit a variety of situations. A large office may need to include a number of possible configurations to allow for changing work conditions. The same may apply to a domestic arrangement, where a home office reverts to 'domestic duties' at the weekend.

Computers and technological advances have certainly been instrumental in changing the design of offices. However, along with these advances, our expectations of how we work have increased dramatically. Natural light, ventilation and accommodation have become important factors in office design. With computers, spaces may be considerably smaller than those provided in the past. But there has been an increase in the services and facilities provided. Many offices now include breakout spaces, often with a full kitchen or kitchenette provided. In many cases, there are also informal reading areas for staff.

There has also been a rethink in the design of waiting rooms. Today, reception areas offer a sense of arrival as well as comfort for clients. Some offices take on the appearance of a five-star hotel, complete with armchairs and sweets on the table. However, while there are a variety of office styles shown in this book, from the more traditional to the more experimental, each has its own distinct signature, one that is rarely duplicated. Staff not only enjoy working in a unique space, but also appreciate the identity conferred on them by working in these spaces. For those of you who still work in traditional office spaces, with a view to a blank wall, reading this book will undoubtedly lead you to rethink your own workspace.

CURVES

ARCHITEKTONIC

Photography by Darren Lunny

THIS ELONGATED OFFICE SPACE HAS ONE MAIN VIEW: THE RAILWAY YARDS DIRECTLY OPPOSITE. A LARGE FLOOR-TO-CEILING WINDOW IS THE ONLY SOURCE OF NATURAL LIGHT IN THIS 1920S CITY BUILDING. 'ORIGINALLY THERE WAS FAUX TIMBER PANELLING ON THE WALLS AND A SUSPENDED CEILING. THE SPACE FELT CAVE-LIKE,' SAYS ARCHITECT JOBURT BETADAM, THE DIRECTOR OF THE PRACTICE ARCHITEKTONIC.

Stained carpet was removed to reveal timber floorboards and the off-formed concrete ceiling was exposed and painted white. To create a sense of width across the office, the few enclosed offices feature floor-to-ceiling glass walls/doors. Working closely with the company Schiavello, there is a strong curvilinear theme in the joinery and the interior space. 'Curves feature strongly in our work. They add an organic quality to the space. Rectilinear lines tend to create a more regimental feel in a workplace,' says Betadam.

Following this theme, the reception area is elliptical in shape. And even the crinkled red laminate counter is curved. 'We can see who has just arrived, but it also creates some privacy,' says architect Owen Meade, who worked closely

with Betadam. A built-in curved bench in the meeting area was designed to overlook the railway yards. Clients can discuss their plans at bar level, or alternatively over coffee around the table.

At Architektonic, there's no hierarchical arrangement of offices. The staff can either use the enclosed spaces or work from their station in the open plan office. 'Equality for the staff has always been an important issue. Everyone is accessible here. But we've also allowed for privacy,' says Meade, who illustrates the point by pulling down an awning adjacent to the front meeting area. 'When the spaces are right, creativity and productivity can flourish,' he says.

FLINDERS STREET

ON THE EDGE

H20

Photography by Trevor Mein

DESIGNED BY H20 ARCHITECTS TIM HURBURGH, MARK O'DWYER AND SOFIA ANAPLIOTIS, THIS BUILDING'S BRIGHT ORANGE CONCRETE FAÇADE IS NOT THE TYPE NORMALLY ASSOCIATED WITH A GOVERNMENT AUTHORITY. HEADQUARTERS OF THE VICTORIAN STATE EMERGENCY SERVICE (SES) AND THE SES'S CENTRAL REGIONAL DIVISION, THIS EXTRAORDINARY NEW BUILDING ABUTS A NETWORK OF FREEWAYS.

Speeding cars cut a swathe through every outlook within the building. In fact, darting cars was a strong influence in the design. 'We wanted to create a sense of movement within the building,' says Anapliotis. 'We looked at what the SES does. They continually respond to disasters. There's always that sense of danger, of hovering on the brink of something,' she adds.

Designed to accommodate sixty staff, with the possibility of future extensions, the site has two street frontages and separate entrances for the two departments within the SES. The functions within each section were carefully articulated to the designers. 'There's the administration component, the crisis co-ordination role and the educational role. The building also had to be

able to service vehicles and support the organisation's communication systems,' says Hurburgh. 'Volunteers account for a significant part of the SES staff. It was important to also create a building that volunteers could identify with, an "esprit de corps",' he adds.

The issue of noise emissions from multiple freeways and the constant need for fresh air were important factors to be considered from the start of the design. The curvature of the windows reduces the sound entering the building. And to channel the air, without opening a single window, vents, in the form of a slatted aluminium louvred wall on the ground floor, allow fresh air to move under the building and through the floor on the level above.

The SES offices (Victorian Headquarters) are divided into three components. There's a large open office. There is the interstitial zone, with some closed and open offices. And the third component consists of more fully enclosed conference and training rooms, leading off one of the longest corridors ever designed (approaching 70 metres). Instead of one long shotgun corridor that appears to go on indefinitely, the architects chose to carefully manipulate the elongated spaces, creating indentations along the way. As Anapliotis says, 'We wanted to create nooks for people to stop and talk informally. They're like pockets that slow down the journey'.

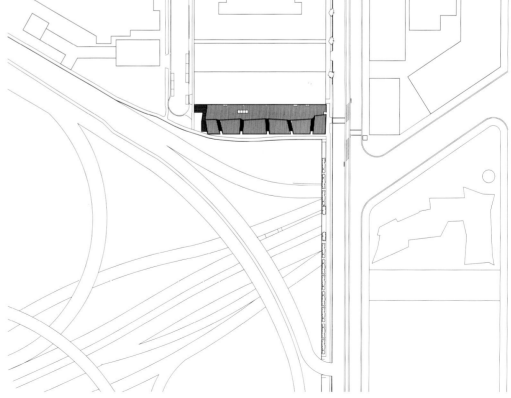

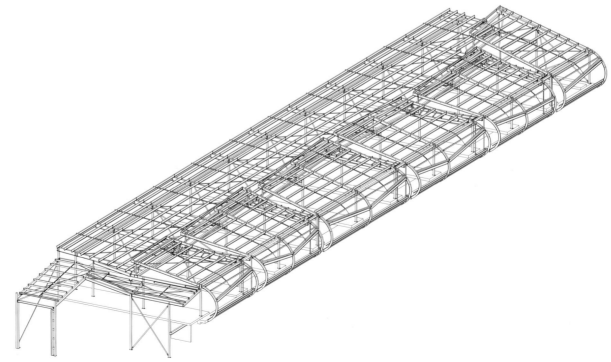

THE FEEL OF A CAMPUS

GEYER

Photography by Shannon McGrath

A CAMPUS-STYLE ENVIRONMENT, RATHER THAN A TRADITIONAL OFFICE, WAS THE MODEL FOR THIS NEW BUILDING. DESIGNED AS A CONTACT CENTRE, THE STRATEGY WAS TO ALLOW THE STAFF TO DEVELOP AS A TEAM.

The building features an interior by Geyer. There is approximately 3000 square metres of floor space on each level. With the first four levels set aside for car parking, the remaining levels focus around a central atrium. 'We wanted to create a different ambience on each level,' says Kelly Hall, a senior interior designer with the practice. The space is designed in three different zones: noisy, eating and the quiet zones (two floors for each type). There is a mixture of zones on each level to allow staff to freely interact.

The first level, after proceeding through a discrete entrance/reception area, is defined as noisy, irrespective of whether there's a crowd (accommodating up to 200 people) or a small gathering. Surrounding the staff are glazed walls, forming an 18-metre-high atrium. 'The space can be used for celebrations or announcements. Whatever the function, we want to make sure the space can change and evolve,' says Hall. Surrounding the void are seemingly endless staircases that wrap around the space. Made of granite (treads), steel and glass, the design includes Juliet-style balconies on every alternative level. These balconies also act as small and informal meeting places.

The 'eating areas', located on the sixth and ninth floors, include a bright laminate kitchen and carpets. As with the other levels, Geyer installed large pendant-style lighting, using different colours to identify the various functions. In contrast to the eating areas, the 'quieter zones', are more sparsely furnished to reduce the number of staff gathering. 'It's a chill-out zone. Staff can sit and read a book or a magazine. The emphasis is on comfort,' says Hall. In sharp contrast to the quiet zones, there are designated floors that allow staff the opportunity to play low-tech games, shoot some pool or play on the pinball machines.

But it's not all play. There are hundreds of workstations. 'One of the main challenges was to cater for changing numbers,' says Hall. And from the start, Geyer was keen to identify the work styles of staff. Some people might be on the phone all day. Others might require more space for meetings. Devising the right footprint for a workstation was as important as locating the right space on each level. As Hall says, 'The design encourages people to interact. It also suggests to them when it's appropriate to keep your voice down'.

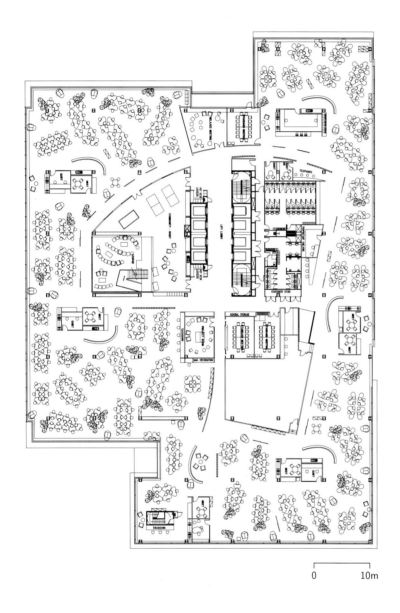

0   10m

INTO A NEW MILLENNIUM

WILLIAMS BOAG PTY LTD ARCHITECTS

Photography by Tony Miller

THIS 1980S BUILDING CARRIED THE HALLMARKS OF THE DECADE: GLASS BRICKS, A STEEL PIPE HAND RAILING AND EVERY POSSIBLE SHADE OF MUSHROOM AVAILABLE. HOWEVER, THE BUILDING'S REDEEMING FEATURES INCLUDE A LARGE ATRIUM (8 METRES IN HEIGHT) AND IT IS ALSO RELATIVELY SPACIOUS, COVERING 1700 SQUARE METRES OVER THREE LEVELS.

The eighties have been dragged into the new millennium thanks to Williams Boag Architects. While the façade was left intact, the interior was completely reworked. The architects were keen to provide direction to the reception area on the first level. It was a long passage that didn't appear to go anywhere. The walls were painted white and the entrance was covered with powder coated metal panels, in yellow and grey. Built-in lighting panels now ensure that the path to the reception is clearly visible.

As the original concrete planter boxes in the atrium could not be removed (they act as structural support for the car park below), the multi-level boxes were concealed with metallic charcoal powder steel sheets. 'Originally the 80s idea was to create a forest. Staff would think they were visiting an exotic place rather than being at work,' says architect Catherine Ramsay

of Williams Boag. The new covered podiums were ideal for Blackwell Publishing Asia, the company occupying the building, to display publications.

The building includes a boardroom that can change in size according to the number of people attending a meeting or function. Concealed behind a large sliding door, the room is framed by a folding fabric-covered wall. On the other side of the wall are canteen facilities for staff. The enclosed rooms adjacent to the open plan offices were also designed with flexibility in mind. In some offices, timber battens provide subtle screening. For others, including the managerial and the director's offices, completely glazed walls create a sense of accessibility for staff. 'There's an emphasis on team work in publishing, so it's important to make the right links and connections,' says Ramsay.

A NEW FRONTIER

ARCHITEKTONIC

Photography by John Gollings

THIS HERITAGE LISTED BUILDING, PREVIOUSLY A BANK, IS IMBUED WITH ALL THE EMBELLISHMENTS OF THE VICTORIAN PERIOD: SOARING CEILINGS, EXTENSIVE TIMBER PANELLING AND ORNATE STAINED GLASS WINDOWS. WHILE THIS LAVISH INTERIOR WAS APPRECIATED BY FRONTIER ECONOMICS, THERE WAS A DESIRE TO CREATE A CONTEMPORARY ENVIRONMENT, ONE THAT WOULD BETTER SUIT THE CLIENT'S BUSINESS. THE LARGE SPACES AND ORNATE 5-METRE CEILINGS WERE INSPIRING. HOWEVER, THE CLIENTS REQUIRED A LESS OVERWHELMING SPACE. 'IT WAS FAIRLY INTIMIDATING FOR BOTH STAFF AND CLIENTS,' SAYS ARCHITECT JOBURT BETADAM, THE DIRECTOR OF ARCHITEKTONIC.

One of the strengths of the building is its rigid symmetry and geometry. The design solution had to embrace a sense of symmetry and geometry in order to satisfy the spatial and aesthetic considerations inherent in the existing form. The intrinsic qualities of the space needed to be preserved such that there was no opportunity for the new tenancy to actually make physical contact with any of the existing building fabric.

A grand building with a grand entrance leading to the space required a sensitive architectural solution for the fit between the old and the new

to be viable. The new internal walls had to reach out to the ceiling without touching it. Architektonic designed a new reception area/office, which features its own floating cantilevered roof. 'It creates a screen or a veil. It also creates an element of surprise when you walk through the reception area and discover the wealth of period features (including the gold-leaf Corinthian columns),' says Betadam.

Workstation furniture selection further enhanced flow within the space. The curved profiles of the worktops and the flexibility of the selected system meant that multiple

rearrangements were possible. The whiteboards, which double as screen doors, exemplify the flexibility of the design. 'We weren't permitted to touch any of the heritage fabric so the joinery (made by Schiavello) had to be freestanding. The curves also provide a contrast to the rigidity of the columns,' says Betadam. Also, in contrast to the formality of the Victorian-style architecture, the designers included a breakout area, where clients and staff can discuss matters more informally. The organic shaped table can be reconfigured and the chairs can be freely moved around the space, described as an oasis.

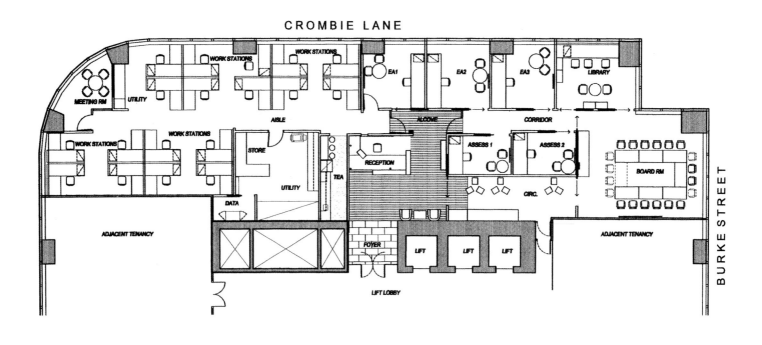

CROMBIE LANE

MEETING RM

UTILITY

WORK STATIONS

WORK STATIONS

EA1

EA2

EA3

LIBRARY

AISLE

ALCOVE

CORRIDOR

WORK STATIONS

WORK STATIONS

STORE

RECEPTION

ASSESS 1

ASSESS 2

BOARD RM

UTILITY

TEA

CIRC.

DATA

ADJACENT TENANCY

ADJACENT TENANCY

FOYER

LIFT

LIFT

LIFT

LIFT LOBBY

BURKE STREET

A LONG RECTILINEAR SPACE

BAENZIGER COLES

Photography by Bryn Holton

DESIGNED FOR RECRUITMENT COMPANY SHL, THIS LONG RECTILINEAR SPACE ENJOYS NATURAL LIGHT FROM ONLY ONE SIDE OF THE BUILDING. WHILE THE MORNING LIGHT ENTERS THE OFFICES AND THE MAIN BOARDROOM ON THE PERIMETER, THE INTERNAL ROOMS WERE LESS THAN IDEAL.

While architects Baenziger Coles were unable to change the footprint within the city building, they were able to design a flexible floor plan that allowed as much natural light into the space as possible. To divide the offices, the designers incorporated large sliding doors. A film was placed on the doors at knee height and just below head height to create privacy when the offices are being used. However, on the door to the boardroom, the film covers the entire door. 'It's a boardroom. It's a meeting room and it's also used for training staff,' says Bryn Holton, the interior designer with Baenziger Coles. When the meeting is informal or not used at all, the glass door is left open. Natural light is then allowed to filter into the reception area, which occupies one of the darkest positions on the floor.

To further create a sense of light in the reception area, Baenziger Coles created a 'dark outline' immediate past the front door. Bluestone flooring, framed with a charcoal navy wall, provides a welcoming mat. And in contrast to this dark entry, the reception is well lit. The red wall behind the reception counter illuminates the space. The reception area also creates a division to the offices. Immediately behind reception is a small breakout area. There are a few stools, a bar fridge (enclosed) and a place to connect a laptop. 'This area is used by candidates waiting to be tested. Alternatively, it's used by staff who are taking a break between sessions,' says Holton.

While the rectilinear design makes the spaces appear to go on indefinitely, it is quite a compact office. Apart from the boardroom, there are three testing rooms and two smaller internal rooms. There's also a small library adjacent to the boardroom. However, the space feels significantly larger and lighter.

THE RIGHT MESSAGE

GRAY PUKSAND

Photography by Shania Shegedyn

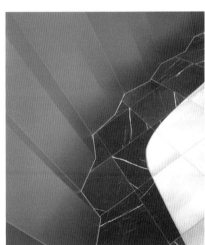

SUBURBAN OFFICE FIT-OUTS TEND TO ERR ON THE CAUTIOUS
SIDE. WORKSTATIONS ARE SPACED AT REGULAR INTERVALS ON
EVERY FLOOR AND CORRIDORS ARE STRAIGHT AND NARROW.
BUT THIS DESIGN FOR INTERNATIONAL MEDICAL SUPPLIERS
SMITH + NEPHEW SIGNALS A CHANGE OF PRACTICE.

Designed by Gray Puksand Architects, the brief from Smith + Nephew was fairly open. They had come from fairly standard office accommodation and wanted something more directional. Designed for 120 staff, the office area intentionally steered away from the hierarchical approach of many organisations. The focus was on strengthening team relationships. In particular, the facility had to include a large area for staff training. Central to the design is a large conference/training room, which adjoins a larger canteen and kitchen area. 'The doors can be pulled back to create one large space for a group. Alternatively, the conference space can be enclosed,' says Puksand. Keen to break down the severity of the office corridors and to suggest something new, Gray Puksand's partitions take the form of concertina-shaped glass.

The galley-style kitchen area, which forms an integral part of the design, is atypical of the suburban office kitchen. The architects chose metallic laminates for the kitchen cupboards and orange colour-backed glass for splashbacks. Even the lime green walls encasing the kitchen put a new spin on the humble canteen. 'The walls are like a key hole. They're ambiguous windows and add a sense of transparency to the office,' says Puksand.

Visitors to the office are ushered to a waiting area framed by a concertina-shaped aluminium screen. And instead of carpet under their feet, the flooring is reconstituted stone. 'Our client was concerned the area would receive a considerable amount of cross traffic (there's a large conference room adjacent to the lobby). The idea was to suggest a rug,' says Puksand. A similar shape to the 'rug' is echoed in the skylight directly above.

As Puksand says, 'Smith + Nephew are a progressive company. They wanted to convey an image of being dynamic as well as professional'.

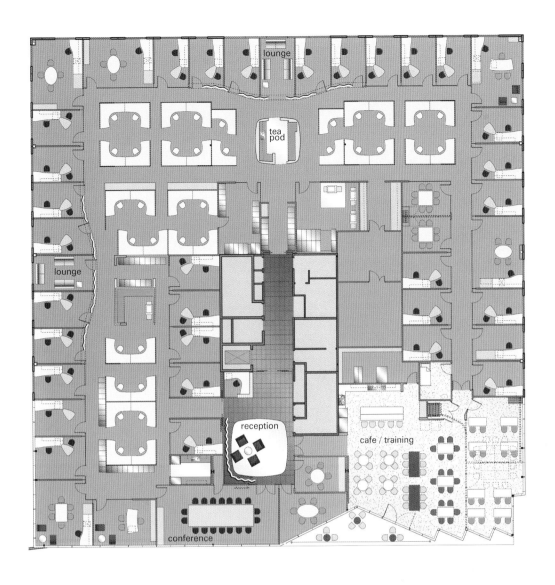

lounge

tea
pod

lounge

reception

cafe / training

conference

A WINTER ROOM

CARR DESIGN

Photography by Earl Carter

THIS HISTORIC BUILDING WAS GUTTED BY FIRE. THE EMPTY SHELL REMAINED UNOCCUPIED FOR SEVERAL YEARS. IT WAS THEN DECIDED TO CONVERT THE SPACE INTO TWO DWELLINGS. AND WHILE THE HISTORIC FAÇADE REMAINED INTACT, THE FIRE PROVIDED AN OPPORTUNITY TO MAKE SOME REAL CHANGES INSIDE THE BUILDING.

As there's a laneway abutting the property, the architects Carr Design inserted a new entry for the second dwelling in the laneway. This created a large uninterrupted space at the front of the house, which is used as a home office. 'Our clients wanted a space where they could work at night. They also wanted a space to use when they weren't at the office,' says architect Sue Carr.

While the townhouse is open plan, the office is located at one end of the house, the kitchen and living areas at the other. There are glimpses of the living areas, as well as the office immediately past the front door. However, when the large floor-to-ceiling pivotal door to the office is closed, there's no clue as to the presence of a room beyond the wall. 'The brief was to include a winter room, a space that could be used as an office or alternatively a place to read a book by the fire,' says Carr. To create a sense of warmth in the office, Carr designed a central fireplace. On each side of the fireplace are ebonised desks, together with shelving. The fireplace not only creates a sense of warmth and focus in the space, but also creates a subtle division when both owners are working together.

The office space isn't large. Measuring approximately 5 by 5 metres, it appears considerably larger when the sunlight reflects on the limestone floors. 'Office spaces don't have to be large. Most things are now stored electronically. There's room for the scanner, the printer and for the owners' laptop computers,' says Carr. And while clients can see into the private realms of the home, they don't need to enter into the private space. A powder room, tucked immediately inside the front entrance, allows clients to remain in the front section of the home.

HOME AND OFFICE

CARR DESIGN

Photography by Shannon McGrath

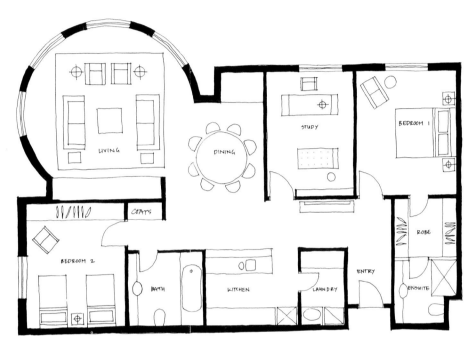

THE OWNERS OF THIS HOME AND OFFICE SPEND MUCH OF THEIR TIME TRAVELLING. THEY REQUIRED SOMETHING THAT COULD BE SIMPLY SHUT DOWN WHEN THEY WEREN'T IN TOWN AND CAME ACROSS THIS THREE-BEDROOM APARTMENT ON THE EDGE OF THE CITY. WHILE THE SPACE WAS ADEQUATE (APPROXIMATELY 100 SQUARE METRES), THE INTERIOR WAS DATED. AND THERE WASN'T A SEPARATE STUDY.

Instead of segmenting the large open plan living and dining area and creating a study, the architects, Carr Design, converted one of the bedrooms into a study. Double layered blinds were installed in the study and the main living areas, one sheer layer, the other a block out. 'Our clients wanted to be able to shut things up entirely when they leave,' says architect Sue Carr.

While the study provides a more private setting to work in, the dining room and living areas are also functional. Neutral finishes were used throughout including American walnut for the

joinery. For the office, Carr design selected an office table designed by JM Frank. The table, designed in two parts, can be extended if additional space is required. 'It's quite a compact space. It's important to use furniture that offers flexibility,' says Carr.

While the apartment functions as a comfortable home, it also incorporates a welcoming office space. 'Today the edges are quite blurred between the home and office. It's partly to do with the laptop. People are also working at different times. Often there's no need to be at an office at nine in the morning,' says Carr.

A SMALL GEM

NEIL + IDLE ARCHITECTS

Photography by Trevor Mein

THIS SMALL OFFICE ON THE EDGE OF TOWN IS A PLAYFUL
ADDITION TO THE STREET. ACTUALLY, IT'S SIMPLY A 1980S
OFFICE BUILDING THAT HAS BEEN REDESIGNED. 'WE CHIPPED
OFF THE MOULDINGS FROM THE FAÇADE AND SIMPLY ADDED A
NEW STEEL CANOPY,' SAYS CAMERON NEIL FROM NEIL + IDLE
ARCHITECTS.

The client, a medical communications company, with offices interstate, required a new office, together with accommodation for interstate managers. The ground floor became the office area and car parking. The second floor was converted into two apartments, one for the on-site manager, the other, the smaller of the two, for the interstate manager. The self-contained smaller apartment can be connected to the larger apartment by simply leaving the door open. 'It saves time and it's more familiar than staying in a hotel,' says Neil.

The office area was designed for four to six full-time staff. Sales staff occupy the front area of the office, while technical staff assemble equipment at the rear of the building. Concealed behind a curved aubergine partition wall at the front of the office are four workstations. As a result, clients entering the office can proceed directly to the conference area, without disturbing staff who may be working. The conference area resembles a space-aged module. The space envelops the occupants with a curved wall and ceiling. 'They wanted a high-tech feeling. It's appropriate to the equipment they produce. But the shape also lends a dynamic quality to the space,' says Neil.

While Neil + Idle design large office fit-outs, the smaller ones allow for more adventurous design. In this case, the large timber door to the conference room was designed to match the joinery in the reception area. As Neil says, 'They wanted a strong statement in the design. It's like the company. They're continually looking for new solutions'.

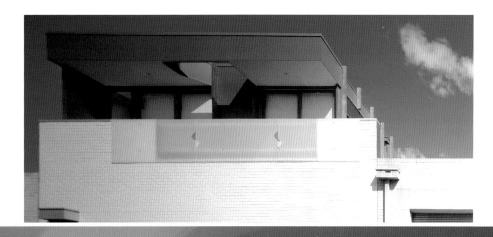

CREATING A STORM

BLIGH VOLLER NIELD

Photography by Dianna Snape

PREVIOUSLY AN OLD WAREHOUSE, THIS BUILDING IS NOW HOME TO STORM, A GRAPHIC DESIGN PRACTICE. BUILT OVER THREE LEVELS, THE SPACE IS SIMILAR TO MANY TERRACE HOMES. AND WHILE THE ORIGINAL SPACE MAY HAVE BEEN SUITABLE AS A HOME, IT WASN'T GOING TO WORK AS AN OFFICE. 'THE STAIRCASE CUT ACROSS THE SECOND LEVEL. CLIENTS WOULD HAVE TO WALK THROUGH THE OFFICE AND DISRUPT WORK. THE FIRST THING THAT HAD TO BE ADDRESSED WAS THE LOCATION OF THE STAIRCASE,' SAYS ARCHITECT BILL DOWZER OF BLIGH VOLLER NIELD.

A key element of the design process was assessing the way staff worked. Because much of the work is done in teams, the design necessitated creating an 'eye of the storm'. The second level became the eye or hub of the office. The central module, with curved sides and sheer drapes, dissects the main office area. The space is divided between the production side (with cutting and layout benches) and the creative component. 'The module is similar to a conversation lounge. It's a place for the team to meet in larger groups or alternatively for clients to discuss their ideas,' says Dowzer.

Placing the main work area on the second level also meant that staff would not have to continually be climbing several flights of stairs.

Bligh Voller Nield also provided a number of places for clients to meet. The reception desk on the ground floor extends to form a bar complete with a couple of bar stools. While the number of treads in the staircase appears daunting from the entrance, the light from windows on the third level draws people into the building. 'It's like a journey. We wanted to create a sense of anticipation as soon as you walked in the front door,' says Sharon Francis, the design architect for the project.

Clients can now pass the main work area on the second level and discover the dynamic environment above. On the top level, the entire site can be fully appreciated. On one side of the office are views of the city, billboards and traffic darting across freeways. On the other side are leafy views towards the street. Even though the third level has been carefully divided into kitchen, meeting area and boardroom, when the doors of the boardroom are kept open, there's a broad vista over the city.

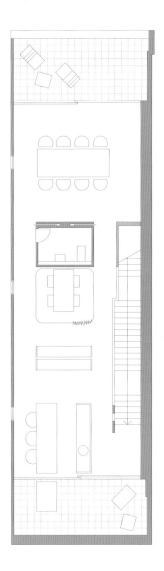

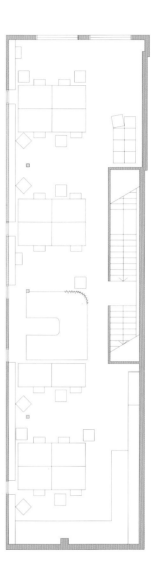

AS OPEN AS IT GETS

BLIGH VOLLER NIELD

Photography by John Van Gemert

THIS OPEN PLAN OFFICE IN THE CITY IS AS OPEN AS IT GETS. THERE ARE FEW, IF ANY, DIVISIONS. THE ONLY PRIVATE SPACE IS THE BATHROOM. 'OUR PREVIOUS OFFICE WAS QUITE HIERARCHICAL. WE FOUND THAT PEOPLE DIDN'T MOVE FROM THEIR OFFICE,' SAYS ARCHITECT BILL DOWZER OF BLIGH VOLLER NIELD.

Located in a 1920s building, this large space, approximately 470 square metres, was previously used as a gallery. When Bligh Voller Nield moved in, they were keen to retain the open space for their own offices. One of the few insertions into the space took the form of shelves for the library. The shelves also conceal the more utilitarian aspects of the practice, the sample boards, materials and the photocopying machines.

While a partition at the entrance partially screens the work area at the front of the practice, most of the office is on view. Instead of workstations for the thirty staff, there are four large tables. The computer screens are one of the few demarcations on the tables. 'Staff move around the office at least three to four times a

year. It depends on the project they're working on and who they are working with,' says architect Jane Williams. In a matter of a few hours, staff can disconnect their computers and take their laptops to a different table. 'If people become too territorial, we know it's time to move them to another space,' says Dowzer. And while some people may find the open plan confronting, the layout reflects the firm's approach to work. 'Everyone needs to know what's going on in the office, even if they're not directly involved,' he adds.

A conference area at the front of the office is screened from the main office area. Sheer silver curtains, framing two conference areas, can be drawn or left open. Green carpet, which forms a curve up the wall, is used to pin up work and

discuss schemes. 'We have a strong culture of design review in our office,' says Dowzer. Clients' comments that the conference area looks like a putting green are reinforced by a putting iron and golf ball in one corner. 'It does have a sense of the outdoors,' says Williams.

When the conference areas are not being used, the curtains are drawn back. The space then combines with the reception area for larger functions. The tables also fold up and can be packed away. As Dowzer says, 'We wanted the spaces to be flexible. There's an area for clients to wait. But if the area isn't being used, it also doubles for quick informal meetings'.

AHEAD OF ITS TIME

DENTON CORKER MARSHALL ARCHITECTS

Photography by Willem Rethmeier, Scott Francis,
James Cant, Earl Carter and John Gollings

THIS OFFICE ON THE EDGE OF THE CITY COULD EASILY BE
MISSED. A LARGE BLANK CONCRETE WALL FACES THE STREET
AND IT COULD EASILY BE MISTAKEN FOR A HIGH SECURITY BANK
VAULT. LIKEWISE, PAST THE FRONT DOOR, THERE ARE FEW
CLUES TO THE BUILDING'S FUNCTION.

It is actually the office of Garry Emery Design, a graphic design practice. Designed in 1984 by Denton Corker Marshall Architects, there were and still are few comparisons to this extraordinary building. The staircase, which resembles an Escher lithograph, appears to go nowhere. Instead of the large glass front doors that lead to a reception foyer, clients face a staircase that leads in three directions.

'One of the staircases narrows and disappears into a wall. Another runs out of headroom. It's the staircase with the granite treads and handrails that delivers you to the offices,' says architect John Denton. 'The staircase is about disruption, while the offices above have a sense of order and serenity. It's about putting opposites together and challenging peoples' perceptions,' says designer Garry Emery. 'We didn't want a front office with the reception area

strongly delineated. It's a more egalitarian area. Our staff are our product and they're on show,' he adds.

To create a balance of working conditions in the office, a series of pod-like capsules were inserted into the open space with its original sawtooth ceiling. One pod functions as the library. Another pod is used as a more private conference room. Rather than the space being carved up like many offices of the time, this office can easily be read as one large picture. 'Its longevity is due to the integrity of the design. There wasn't a series of compromises,' Denton says.

And while the façade creates a sense of mystery, the rear elevation opens to a large sunlit terrace with city views.

SENSE OF DISCOVERY

WOODS BAGOT

Photography by Trevor Mein

Cornwell Design, a graphic design company, started in business ten years ago from a basement down a laneway. Now with twenty staff, the practice required larger offices. 'We still wanted to recognise the firm's early days,' says architect and interior designer Nik Karalis of Woods Bagot, who located the entrance to the new office down a laneway. 'There's a sense of discovery. It also creates a journey for clients,' he adds.

Formerly a warehouse, the 400-square-metre building still contains a sawtooth ceiling. Inside, the spaces and the materials used are quite simple. Concrete appears in the floors and in the reception counter. The only other materials used are painted MDF, laminate and Perspex. However, while the materials are simple, they have been used to maximum effect. Perspex shelving surrounds the main work area, which consists of tables.

There are no divisions between staff. 'The arrangement isn't dissimilar to how we worked as students. The emphasis is on what they do. It's a dynamic studio and clients can see how the studio works,' says Karalis. The laminate and Perspex shelves were designed for books and anything else belonging to staff, such as people's lunch boxes. 'It creates an interesting texture and another layer to the space,' says Karalis.

In contrast to the open work areas, Woods Bagot designed an enclosed capsule, simply painted MDF. There's a presentation room, two strategy rooms and a separate cut and paste room. Light enters into this space via the skylights in the ceiling. The solid black core also accentuates the roof profile. As Karalis says, 'The design is a response to what they do. It's about the creation of ideas'.

A DESIGN CLASSIC

BATES SMART

Photography by Trevor Mein

DESIGNED BY BATES SMART & MCCUTCHEON IN 1958, THIS ELEGANT SKYSCRAPER WAS THE FIRST HIGH RISE BUILDING IN THE CITY. IT WAS ALSO ONE OF THE FIRST PROJECTS TO INCORPORATE A PRECAST CONCRETE FLOOR SYSTEM. INTERESTINGLY, THIS GLASS CURTAIN-WALLED BUILDING IS NOW OCCUPIED BY THE ARCHITECTS WHO DESIGNED THE BUILDING (OCCUPYING THE 6TH AND 7TH FLOORS).

When Bates Smart moved into the building a couple of years ago, it was a warren of office partitions. Even though the lift core is designed to one side of the floor plate, the partitions used in the previous office eliminated the city views on either side of the building. The ceiling, an engineering feat, had also been covered with a false ceiling. However, the generous floor space spread over the two levels (950 square metres per floor) was appreciated by the architects, as was the original detailing that appeared throughout the building. The lobby for example, although refurbished, still contains terrazzo flooring and dark slatted timber walls.

Previous workstations and partitions were completely removed from the offices and the windows were freed up. Staff work tables, together with open conference tables, occupy the central core. And even the directors' offices, encased with glass, were designed away from the windows. Instead of workstations adjacent to the windows, there is a continuous line of drawers. In the public area, these shelves are used to display objects d'art and in the work areas, to spread out work. 'We tried to keep the space as open as possible. We didn't want anyone to own the view,' says interior designer Jeffrey Copolov, a co-director of the practice. And while the directors have their own offices, there's a conference table in each for staff to use.

At either end of the space are separate pavilions. At one end is the boardroom, and the other end of the office is the kitchen area. Built-in banquette style seating provides for extra seating and there's even a built-in magazine rack. 'The two modules are like book ends,' says Copolov.

The interior spaces now capture the strong sharp lines of the building. Designed for up to one hundred staff, the office allows for a continuous flow of traffic. And like the views over the city, this is now completely unimpeded.

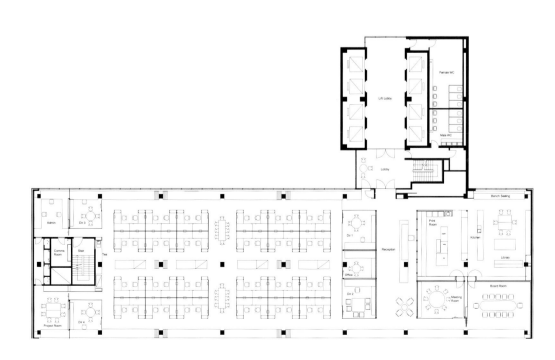

AN EYE FOR DETAIL

JAN MANTON ARCHITECTS
Photography by James Grant

WHEN YOU ENTER THIS HOME, YOU GET THE IMMEDIATE IMPRESSION THAT EVERYTHING IS EXACTLY RIGHT. FROM THE PROPORTIONS OF THE ROOMS TO THE FINISHES, EVERYTHING IS IMPECCABLE. DESIGNED BY ARCHITECT MICHAEL JAN AS HIS OWN HOME, THE DESIGN INCLUDES A LARGE HOME OFFICE FOR BOTH HIM AND HIS PARTNER.

Downstairs is the formal living area, dining and kitchen area. Upstairs, there are two bedrooms and a central study. The main bedroom and ensuite is at one end of the house, the guest's bedroom at the other.

While the house is presently designed with two bedrooms, there's an option of dividing up the spacious study into two smaller rooms. However, for Jan's requirements, the large study is ideal. Jan included a large window seat in the projected window, which extends the entire length of the second storey. 'It's like an indoor–outdoor room,' says Jan, who demonstrates with the touch of a button, the

versatility of the window. The aluminium 'reefing' blinds can be fully retracted and the glass shug-styled windows can be drawn right back to allow sun and fresh air into the home. When the windows and blinds are retracted, the feeling is comparable to sitting on a veranda. The sound of water from the pond below adds to the sense of the outdoors. A sense of transparency extends to the walls separating the study from the adjacent bedrooms. Glass partitions above the window seat create a sense of continuous space.

The two study areas, although sharing the same space, are quite different in style. Jan prefers contemporary design, while his partner prefers a

more traditional approach. A classic high-backed winged chair is in contrast to Jan's more streamlined furniture. However, while these two styles are quite distinct, continuous bookshelves that line the rear wall unify the space. A delightful collection of objects and artefacts in the study also creates a unique ambience to the place. As Jan says, 'We don't just use the study for work. It's also a place to retreat at the end of the day'.

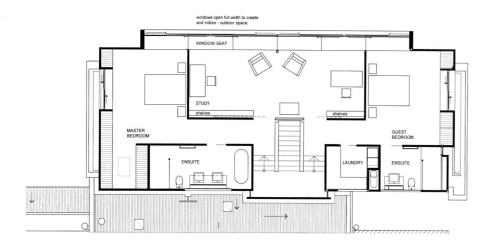

windows open full width to create
and indoor - outdoor space

WINDOW SEAT

STUDY

shelves   shelves

MASTER
BEDROOM

GUEST
BEDROOM

ENSUITE   LAUNDRY   ENSUITE

A 1970S CLASSIC

JOHN KENNY ARCHITECT
Photography by John Kenny

DESIGNED IN 1975 BY ARCHITECT JOHN KENNY, THIS STRIKING TIMBER HOME COMPRISES FOUR DISTINCT MODULES. THERE'S THE KITCHEN, LIVING AREAS AND BEDROOM MODULES. AND THE HOME OFFICE IS TREATED AS A SEPARATE MODULE. THE MODULES WERE DESIGNED ACCORDING TO THE SITE, ACCESSIBILITY, ORIENTATION AND PRIVACY.

The home office, approximately 55 square metres in size, is lined in celery top pine and features a dramatic 5-metre-high ceiling with a mezzanine. 'I was influenced by Alvar Alto. I've always loved his pragmatic use of materials and the way they're used simply and honestly,' says Kenny. Treated as a separate module, the study can be closed off from the family home. There's a door to the kitchen and a separate entrance to the office from the front courtyard. 'It means that clients don't have to go through the house. The office is self-contained, except for bathroom facilities,' says Kenny.

As Kenny has always been a sole practitioner, he felt it was important to locate the office closest to the street. And although it's a quiet inner suburban street, people still walk past. 'It's important to see movement in a street. Working on your own can be an isolating experience. The noise from the street is minimal. But it makes you feel as though you're part of a community,' says Kenny, who enjoys opening the large sliding timber doors, particularly during the warmer months. While there is no air conditioning in the office, there are two sets of sliding doors on the ground level and one on the mezzanine, opening to the front balcony. With the high ceilings and three sets of doors, there is a continual flow of air throughout the space.

While the office is open plan, the mezzanine was included to provide a separate conference area. Informal and simply furnished with a couple of deck chairs, the mezzanine is used by Kenny to see clients. 'It's away from the work area and it's a great place for clients to think about what they want to achieve in their homes,' says Kenny. And while facilities have become more sophisticated in the last thirty years since the house was built, clients can't help but be impressed by these elegant and refined spaces. As Kenny says, 'Most people comment on the tranquillity of the space. Particularly since it's only ten minutes from the city'.

A JOURNEY

STEPHEN JOLSON ARCHITECT PTY LTD

Photography by Tim Griffith

THIS OFFICE, DESIGNED BY ARCHITECT STEPHEN JOLSON, IS
LOCATED IN A SPORTS STADIUM AT FOX STUDIOS. KNOWN AS
THE FRANK HURLEY GRANDSTAND, THE ARCHITECTS WERE
GIVEN LITTLE MORE THAN A SHELL IN WHICH TO CREATE A NEW
OFFICE FOR THE PROMOTIONS DEPARTMENT.

Approximately 280 square metres in area, the shell consisted of concrete floors and exposed services. 'We really had to start from scratch,' says Jolson. As the name implies, 'promotions' includes everything from billboards and pamphlets to cut-out figures. However, while the architects had to allow for all the paraphernalia, their clients, as well as their own aesthetic, suggested a streamlined office.

Entry to the office is quite discreet. Instead of the reception desk (which is located out of sight), staff and clients are greeted with fin-like walls. Varying in distance from 0.5 to 1.4 metres, each fin, measuring 110 mm in width, conceals the display material used by the company. As people walk down the corridor, each display becomes visible. 'There's a hierarchy to the material. The more substantial displays are towards the end of the passage,' says Jolson. The spine-like wall also directs clients to the conference area, which can be screened by glass doors.

An alternate route directs people through an aluminium-lined corridor. This leads to the open plan office areas and lounge area. 'We wanted to create the sense of a journey and also to create a sense of compression,' says Jolson, who designed the office area with soaring 5-metre-high ceilings. And while the views leading to the main office area are enclosed, the end of the tunnel signals spectacular views over the showground. The workstations all feature partitions. But it's not difficult to see above these and take in the panoramic views. Only the two directors' offices have been enclosed. Framed with glass, the occupants of these offices can also enjoy the location.

While the lounge area creates a breakout space for informal staff meetings, it is also used for client meetings. For the architects, creating a sense of order out of all the paraphernalia was crucial. And while detailing is important in any project, it's the planning that is at the forefront of the design. 'It's crucial how the spaces are organised and their relationship to each other,' says Jolson.

STUDIO STYLE

MCBRIDE CHARLES RYAN – ARCHITECTURE + INTERIOR DESIGN

Photography by Louis Petruccelli

THIS STUDIO STYLE OFFICE WAS ORIGINALLY A 1960S CREAM BRICK FACTORY. IT WAS THEN TRANSFORMED INTO A PHOTOGRAPHIC STUDIO AND OFFICE FOR THE OWNER, PHOTOGRAPHER LOUIS PETRUCCELLI. REWORKED IN THE LATE 1980S BY MCBRIDE CHARLES RYAN ARCHITECTS, THIS INNER CITY STUDIO REMAINS A SHARP STATEMENT IN CONTEMPORARY DESIGN.

The brief to the architects was to use one third of the space as offices and two thirds for the studio. 'The studio space had to be flexible. Sometimes room sets are required, while at other times two shoots might need to be scheduled,' says Petruccelli. Long hours aren't unusual in the industry so the interior had to be stimulating. McBride Charles Ryan also had to provide support areas for the studio, such as a dressing room for models, a kitchen, a conference room and a leisure deck.

Security was an issue and the architects were urged to restrain the external public gestures. However, once inside the building, the senses are activated. The double-storey glass brick wall

used in the façade was an ideal barrier to a harsh urban environment, allowing diffused light to penetrate the interior. The perforated steel staircase that cantilevers into the double-storey void also diffuses the internal light.

The office and conference area were designed on the mezzanine level. Frosted glass tables, separated by perforated steel walls and shelves create a sense of enclosure in the open plan office. When the velvet curtains are pulled back to reveal the studio below, numerous tasks can be carried out by Petruccelli at the same time. 'I can literally sit at my desk on the phone and take in the action below.'

'The two areas are in a way a contrast of each other. The strong graphic lines and hard terrazzo flooring in the public area is cushioned by the soft navy velvet drapes and carpeted floors of the office,' says Debbie-Lyn Ryan, the firm's interior designer.

As the building covers the entire site, outdoor spaces were created in the form of a roof deck and a small front balcony that overlooks the street. The zincalum outcrop is the ideal place for staff to unwind at the end of the day. As Petruccelli says, 'It's terrific to feel part of the streetscape and not feel closed off, particularly when the days turn into evenings'.

PROGRESSIVE

BBP ARCHITECTS

Photography by Chris Ott

THIS NEW OFFICE FOR ABM PLASTIC PROVIDES THE COMPANY WITH A NEW IMAGE. WHILE THE COMPANY HAD ALWAYS PRIDED ITSELF ON ITS PROGRESSIVE STYLE OF BUSINESS, ITS OFFICES WERE FAR FROM DIRECTIONAL. MANY OF THE COMPANY'S ORIGINAL OFFICES WERE SPREAD OUT IN THE INDUSTRIAL STREET. AND THE EXISTING WAREHOUSE, BUILT IN THE 1960S, REQUIRED REWORKING. SO TO DEAL WITH TWO SEPARATE PROBLEMS, BBP ARCHITECTS RENOVATED THE OLD WAREHOUSE AND CREATED AN IMPRESSIVE NEW OFFICE WING ON THE SAME SITE.

By consolidating the separate offices in the street, the architects were able to create one new building. 'It's their national headquarters. They wanted something that would express their technical advancements in the industry,' says architect David Balestra-Pimpini. 'We were fortunate that the managing director has a strong interest in design,' he adds.

The new offices were designed in steel and glass. However, as one elevation is towards the harshest sunlight, the architects designed a second layer in the form of a perforated steel mesh screen. Located 2 metres from the glazed façade, sunlight filters into the two-storey

building. A pond, running the entire length of the same elevation, adds a sense of tranquillity to the offices on both levels. 'The screen reduces the views to the street and creates a courtyard feel to the offices. It's like an oasis in the centre of an industrial area,' says Balestra-Pimpini.

Inside the office building, visitors are greeted by a double-height void and glazed walls. The double-height space not only creates a sense of transparency, but also makes an important connection to the offices on the second level. The architects used a simple range of materials and kept to a fairly monochromatic colour scheme. The only colours used, orange and

gunmetal grey, articulate the structural assemblage of the building. The company logo is sandblasted on the glass walls.

While the old 1960s warehouse was retained, it was rendered and 'painted out', almost disappearing into the site. The presence of the new building creates little or no distraction.

WORKING FROM HOME

FORM ARCHITECTURE FURNITURE

Photography by Dan Magree

ARCHITECT POLLY BASTOW AND HER PARTNER TONY STUART, A FURNITURE DESIGNER, HAVE ALWAYS PREFERRED WORKING FROM HOME. THERE ISN'T THE PROBLEM OF BEING STUCK IN TRAFFIC AND THE PAIR CAN COME AND GO AS THEY CHOOSE.

Previously, Bastow worked from the 1920s semi-detached home in the suburbs and Stuart made furniture from the 1950s corrugated iron shed in the back yard. That was until the shed burnt down. 'It was the right time to think about building something both of us could use, away from the house, which could be locked up at night,' says Bastow.

As the generous rear garden overlooks a plumbing yard, the couple were able to build two storeys (neighbours were not going to be overlooked). 'We wanted to explore ideas with this project, similar to a laboratory. We definitely didn't want to appear too serious,' says Bastow. The new two-storey office is a

melange of materials. There's the corrugated steel 'slippery-dip' with stripes and a concrete block façade, which appears like the wall of a ruin. 'It's reminiscent of the past shed, even though it's a new design with different materials,' she says. There's also a large canopy over the office, made of cement sheeting, that provides protection from the direct sun.

The ground floor is Stuart's workshop. And upstairs, via a plywood staircase, are a conference area and a space with a large built-in desk for both Bastow and Stuart. The conference area is defined by a curved plywood canopy and with a lime green pod-like wall, which encloses the library, kitchen and

bathroom facilities. Known for their use of recycled materials, the duo were keen to incorporate second hand windows in the office. The Mondrian-style windows, of varying dimensions, are used in a contemporary manner. 'Clients can see how we work. But they can also see how we use materials. It's often easier than having to talk about your work,' says Stuart.

The pet dog named Leda, the company's logo, also features in the workspace. Leda's graphic outline appears on the lime green office wall. As Bastow says, 'It's a calm environment to work in. And it works for us'.

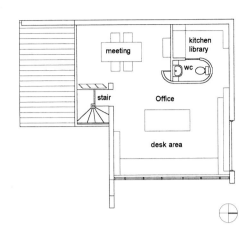

Studio workshop

stair

meeting

kitchen
library

wc

stair

Office

desk area

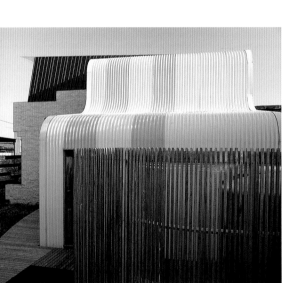

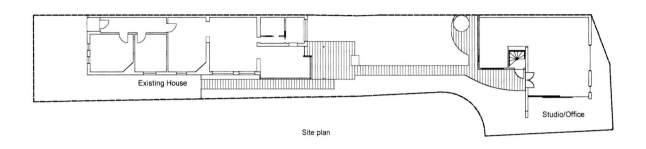

Existing House

Site plan

Studio/Office

GRAPHIC

MELOCCO AND MOORE ARCHITECTS
Photography by Paul Gosney

THIS OFFICE, DESIGNED BY MELOCCO AND MOORE ARCHITECTS, IS FOR NOVA DESIGN ASSOCIATES, GRAPHIC DESIGNERS. LOCATED IN 'GOWINGS', A HISTORIC RETAIL BUILDING IN THE HEART OF THE CITY, THE INTERIOR SPACE WAS CONSIDERABLY LESS ORNATE THAN THE BUILDING'S FAÇADE. 'THE INTERIOR SPACE WAS QUITE RAW. THE ONLY IMPROVEMENT MADE TO THE SPACE WAS POLISHED TIMBER FLOORS. GALVANISED SERVICE TRAYS SUSPENDED FROM THE ROOF (CONCEALING THE SERVICES) HAD ALSO BEEN INSTALLED,' SAYS ARCHITECT DAVID MELOCCO.

As the space is elongated, with restricted views to the street, the architects designed the walls at approximately 2.5 metres, considerably less than the 4-metre-high ceilings. 'We wanted to maintain airflow throughout the office. But we also wanted a sense of privacy,' says Melocco.

The office is essentially divided into two spaces. On one side, with natural light and views to the street, are the workstations for the staff (approximately ten). On the other side of the office are the reception area, conference room, storeroom and director's areas. Dissecting these two areas is a gallery space. The gallery wall, 800 mm in width, acts as a barrier to the open plan

office area. There are no doors to the office area and people walking through simply see vignettes of people working. 'This wall is used to display the company's work over the years,' says Melocco.

While the main conference area is enclosed, the architects designed perforated MDF doors. The large sliding doors were laser-cut and designed to give a sense of privacy while maintaining a visual connection to the gallery and design studio. The lowered ceiling over the conference room table creates a more intimate setting. Because of heritage issues, the existing ceiling was maintained and all services were exposed

(even those seen through the steel trays). 'The walls had to be slipped underneath the hanging trays, so they were given a thickness and depth to become solid objects within the space,' says Melocco.

The directors have their own space, but it was deliberately designed as open plan. Staff can freely move into this space to discuss their ideas. 'We didn't want to create a hierarchy of spaces. But at the same time, there had to be definition. And it had to function as an office'.

CREATING A DIVISION

DOYLE ARCHITECT PTY LTD

Photography by Trevor Mein

WHEN ARCHITECT JUDE DOYLE DECIDED TO RENOVATE HER 1920S HOME, SHE INCLUDED IN THE BRIEF A SEPARATE HOME OFFICE. WITH SMALL CHILDREN, SHE NEEDED HER OWN SPACE WHERE HER ARCHITECTURAL PLANS WOULDN'T BE USED AS DRAWING PAPER. 'I'VE BEEN WORKING FROM HOME FOR THE LAST FEW YEARS. THE RENOVATION WITH THE OFFICE WAS A NATURAL PROGRESSION,' SAYS DOYLE. 'BRUCE (DOYLE'S PARTNER) ALSO WANTED A SPACE FOR HIS EQUIPMENT (HE WORKS IN THE FILM INDUSTRY),' SHE ADDS.

One large extension was designed for the home. Corridors and wasted passageways were eliminated. 'I wanted to be able to see through the entire house as soon as I opened the front door. There are a series of elements to look through. But there's a transparency through to the back yard,' says Doyle.

The western red cedar used for the extension and separate office was selected for its unique qualities. 'It's great to work with and has a wonderful texture. It also has a golden hue,' says Doyle, who combined the timber with simple fibro-cement sheets for the exterior of the building. As an alternative to the back door, there's a continuous wall of glass windows/doors.

Originally, the western red cedar building in the back yard was used as a pottery studio. It then became a garage. When Doyle's second child arrived, it became an office. The timber-clad office, punctuated with a 3-metre-long canteen style window, allows home and work to be separated. A grass knoll, creating a gentle curve in the back yard, provides a subtle division. Should the architecture office expand beyond these premises, the building could be used for anything from guest's quarters to a separate family room.

Inside the office, Doyle incorporated recycled materials. Old wardrobe panels line the office and the shelving came from a 1950s chemist. 'The wardrobe panels came from my parents'

house. It was also built in the 1950s,' says Doyle. While the wardrobe doors are used to add a decorative layer to the office, the shelves from the chemist have a functional use and include space for plans and stationary.

The elongated window in the office allows Doyle to see clients arriving. It also allows her to keep an eye on the children if she's working on the weekend. As Doyle says, 'It's been important to keep the two zones separate. Clients don't have to walk through the house. And the children don't have to come into the office'.

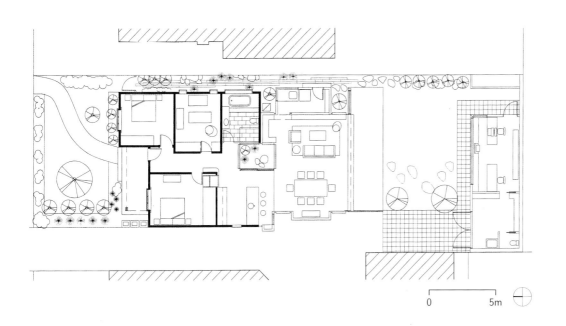

0   5m

ONCE A FACTORY

CRAIG ROSSETTI ARCHITECT
Photography Andrew Ashton

THIS OFFICE, IN AN INDUSTRIAL INNER CITY AREA, WAS PREVIOUS A FITTING AND TURNING FACTORY. BUILT IN 1974 AND CONSTRUCTED IN CONCRETE BLOCKS, GLASS AND WITH A STEEL ROOF, IT'S NOW A SHARE OFFICE FOR AN ARCHITECT, PHOTOGRAPHER, DRAFTSMAN, DEVELOPER AND INTERNET GROUP.

When architect Craig Rossetti moved into the space a couple of years ago, there was little light. Designed as a factory, the building's main feature was a loading bay at the front. 'The building occupied almost the entire site. There was no rear yard and customers walked directly into the space,' says Rossetti, who redesigned the space.

The loading bay was enclosed with a large glass window and a custom-made planter box. The small office adjacent to the bay was retained. However, instead of customers walking through the small office from the street, the entrance was relocated to the side of the building and a new

glass window was inserted into the office. As a reminder of the building's previous use, a car hoist is still embedded into the front wall of the building.

The footprint of the building was marginally reduced. A side garden was planted and the building was reduced by 3.5 metres from the rear boundary. One continuous skylight was inserted to create additional light. The original highlight windows were eliminated and substituted by floor-to-ceiling windows. Light now enters into the space from all directions and the rear courtyard, although small, is appreciated in such a built up location.

While the office is open plan, the front conference room and small office allow for private meetings. Even though these rooms face directly onto the street, translucent glass and a planter box create sufficient privacy. As the office is shared, there is no hierarchy. People come and go and expenses are shared. As Rossetti says, 'Most people find working on their own to be quite lonely. There's always people coming and going. And you never feel as if you're working in a harsh urban environment. There's greenery and a sense of the outdoors'.

DOWN A LANE

BIRD DE LA COEUR ARCHITECTS
Photography by John Gollings

BUILT IN THE 1920S, THIS BUILDING WAS ORIGINALLY USED TO MAKE BISCUITS. A PHOTOGRAPHER THEN MOVED INTO THE BUILDING. AND THE SECOND FLOOR, LEASED BY A THEATRE COMPANY, WAS USED FOR STORAGE. LOCATED IN A LANEWAY BEHIND AN INNER BAYSIDE SHOPPING STRIP, THIS BUILDING IS NOW THE HOME AND OFFICE OF BIRD DE LA COEUR ARCHITECTS.

Architects Vanessa Bird and her partner Neil de la Coeur were looking for a new place which would not only be suitable for work, but also to raise their children. 'We didn't mind that there wasn't a back yard. It's close to parkland and the beach is just a short walk away,' says Bird. Initially the building was gutted completely. The only things that remained were the concrete floor on the upper level, the walls and the roof. The original timber stable door was also retained. The second level was converted in a home and the ground floor into the office.

Behind the stable door, Bird de la Coeur inserted a new glass shop front and created a small reception area. The conference area was simply defined with a heavy stainless steel mesh curtain. 'We bought it from a scrap metal merchant. We think it was originally used in a bakery, like a conveyor belt,' says Bird. And while the curtain is transparent, staff and visitors know when not to enter the space. 'It's a sufficient barrier,' she adds.

As the office is relatively compact, the services such the kitchen and bathroom were tucked into an 'aluminium box' adjacent to the conference area. This box also contains storage, filing cabinets and a switchboard. 'The aluminium is like a wrapping. It separates the more public areas at the front from the work areas,' says Bird. When the conference area isn't being used, it doubles as a larger workspace or for staff to have their lunch. And for the staff, pleasure comes from working in such a light space. The original steel case windows were retained which bring light in from all directions.

There's a sense of arrival, almost delight for clients, who are often surprised to find an office down the laneway. As Bird says, 'Most people are surprised to find us here. There's the sense of discovery'.

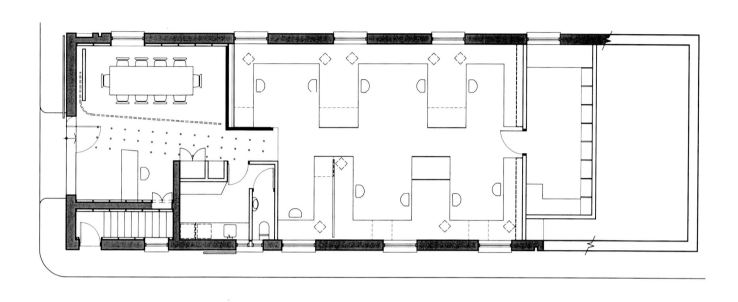

BLURRING THE LINES

ARCHITECTS JOHANNSEN + ASSOCIATES PTY LTD
Photography by Anthony Fretwell

THIS LARGE PRINTING COMPANY, PMP, HAD A NUMBER OF OFFICES SCATTERED AROUND THE CITY. A DECISION TO CONSOLIDATE THE SPACES WAS ALSO THE APPROPRIATE TIME TO THINK ABOUT HOW STAFF COULD BEST WORK TOGETHER. 'THEIR OTHER OFFICES WERE QUITE TRADITIONAL. MANY OF THE OFFICES WERE SEPARATE AND WEREN'T DISTINGUISHABLE FROM EACH OTHER,' SAYS ARCHITECT GABY GERING, A DIRECTOR OF ARCHITECTS JOHANNSEN + ASSOCIATES.

The company's new office is located in a thriving shopping centre. The kitchen, which is adjacent to the meeting rooms, has a domestic feel. Timber has been used and the finishes and fixtures are similar to those found in a domestic kitchen. 'Part of the brief was to improve the social interaction within the company. The idea was to create a sense of familiarity,' says Gering, who has noticed the changes in office design over the last few years. 'Commercial fit-outs have become more domestic and in many cases, domestic projects have a more commercial feel to them. In this instance, we wanted to provide a level of comfort. Staff feel as though it's their own kitchen,' says Gering.

While the kitchen is open to the meeting rooms, it can be closed off entirely. Likewise, the adjacent meeting rooms can be used as one large space or divided into three separate meeting rooms by means of large sliding doors. The main boardroom features timber to create a warmer ambience. And there's a deliberate translucency to the space. The timber is combined with translucent glass and between the two materials, the architects left a gap. People walking past have a sense of what's going on without being directly involved. There are simply glimpses of people in a meeting.

Even though there are several open plan offices spread over the three levels of this building, the brief also required several enclosed offices. But mindful of not wanting to create the same enclosed feeling that staff left behind, the architects included glass walls. They also created larger offices and included small tables as an alternative to the built-in desk. As Gering says, 'The office now doubles as a 'quick meet room'. Offices have lost much of their formality. And for all parties, it's a much more pleasurable way of conducting business'.

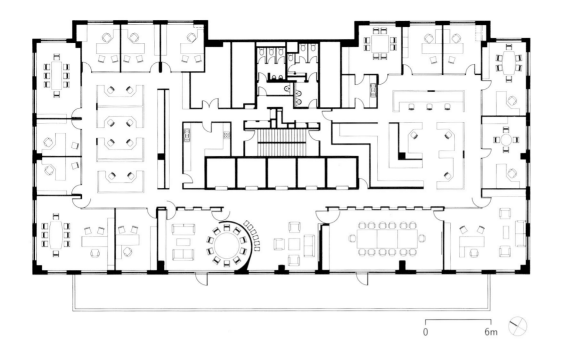

0   6m

TRANSPARENT

JACKSON CLEMENTS BURROWS ARCHITECTS

Photography by John Gollings

LOCATED ON THE EDGE OF THE CITY, THIS WAREHOUSE
ORIGINALLY CONSISTED OF ONE LARGE OPEN SPACE. 'WE
ESSENTIALLY INHERITED A SHELL. BUT THE SPACE IS GENEROUS
AND LIGHT,' SAYS ARCHITECT TIM JACKSON OF JACKSON
CLEMENTS BURROWS ARCHITECTS. DESIGNED FOR A RECORD
COMPANY CALLED ZOMBA RECORDS, THE BRIEF TO THE
ARCHITECTS WAS TO CREATE A 'TRANSPARENT SPACE', WHERE
THE LIGHT COULD INFILTRATE THE CORE OF THE BUILDING.

To allow this to occur, the architects used a domestic stud wall construction system to create the divisions. However, instead of concealing the timber frames with plaster sheets, they used a clear corrugated polycarbonate. Plywood sheeting was then used for the lower portion of the walls (up to 1200 mm). 'It meant that desks could be concealed, allowing for privacy. But the light could still infiltrate the offices,' says Jackson. The architects were also keen to add a decorative layer to the office. 'We found these wallpapers in a second hand store. Most are samples from the 1970s,' says Jackson. The wallpapers add a graphic and colourful stroke to the interior, with the vibrant colours reflecting off the walls.

The utilities in the office are also clearly expressed. The air conditioning and the sprinkler system were left exposed. Even the fluorescent lighting follows the structural beams in the warehouse. 'It was a fairly tight budget. But allowing the elements to be exposed worked with the design'.

At the core of the space is a lounge area and kitchen, together with a distribution and sales office. 'We wanted to create quite an informal space, somewhere where musicians feel comfortable, a place that wasn't intimidating,' says Jackson. While the budget was tight, the sense of space isn't. As Jackson says, 'The owner was keen to provide a work space where his staff would be comfortable. It's not precious. It's a place to enjoy working in'.

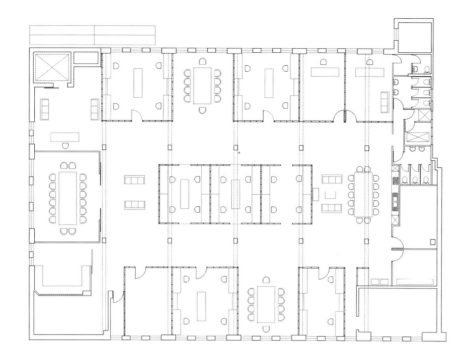

JUST LANDED

MINIFIE NIXON

Photography by Peter Bennetts, Minifie Nixon

DESIGNED BY ARCHITECTS MINIFIE NIXON, THIS EXTRAORDINARY NEW BUILDING APPEARS TO HAVE LANDED FROM ANOTHER GALAXY. ITS STRIKING STAINLESS STEEL FAÇADE IS A SIGNIFICANT ADDITION TO THE VICTORIAN COLLEGE OF THE ARTS IN MELBOURNE, AUSTRALIA. THE EMBOSSED STAINLESS STEEL CONES WERE DERIVED FROM A VORONOI DIAGRAM, USED IN APPLIED MATHEMATICS. 'WE'RE CONSCIOUS OF CERTAIN READINGS. THERE'S ALSO BEEN THE SUGGESTION OF STAR SIGNS, IN THE WAY THE POINTS HAVE BEEN ARRANGED,' SAYS ARCHITECT PAUL MINIFIE.

The brief to the architects was extensive, as numerous functions had to be included in this building. The existing library required additional space. And there was also a need for teaching spaces, additional offices and computer labs for students. 'It was quite a complicated brief. Several of the offices in the adjoining buildings had to be reorganised and access had to be provided to the new spaces,' says Minifie.

On the first level are separate offices, computer labs and the new library, which is linked to the existing library. On the top level, there's an open plan office, which acts as a centre for ideas. Running through the levels is a staircase, slightly skewed, that skims over the library on the

second level. 'This area is an interstitial between the two libraries (one existing, one new). It's also a place where students meet. Circulation was essential. There can be a hundred students in this space at any one time,' says Minifie.

The large open plan area on the top level, known as the Centre for Ideas, features a graphic ceiling with fluorescent lights. The lights connect the dots in the façade, bringing the dynamics of the façade into the interior space. And as the centre is open plan, the architects included perforated plywood to line the walls for acoustic control. Carpet on the floors also reduces the noise level. There is the option of segmenting the space in the future, should this be required.

In contrast to the futuristic façade, the interior spaces are simple and robust. Bright linoleums ensure longevity and the colours add a graphic quality to the space. Clever paint finishes, such as the one used on the staircase (painted from orange to cream) suggest movement within the space, as well as the sunlight's reflection. To bring additional light into the core of this building, the architects used a plastic membrane below the fibreglass ceiling.

This new building represents an important addition to Victoria's premier arts school and brings it well and truly into the twenty-first century and beyond.

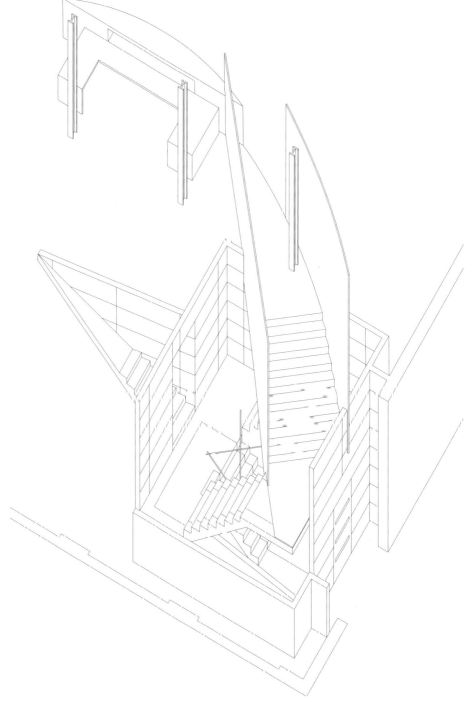

WELL CONNECTED

INARC ARCHITECTURE

Photography by Peter Clarke

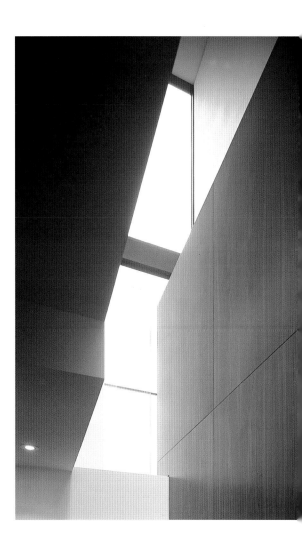

THIS THREE-STOREY TOWNHOUSE ON THE EDGE OF TOWN WAS COMPLETELY GUTTED BY INARC ARCHITECTS FOR CLIENTS WHO WERE AFTER A HOME/OFFICE. EVEN THOUGH IT WAS BUILT FAIRLY RECENTLY, IN THE MID-1990S, THE THREE STOREYS FAILED TO CONNECT AND THE ROOMS, PARTICULARLY ON THE GROUND FLOOR, WERE NOT SUITABLY ORIENTATED. 'IT DIDN'T WORK AS A HOUSE. AND IT WORKED EVEN LESS AS A HOME OFFICE,' SAYS ARCHITECT RENO RIZZO.

One of the key elements of the new design is the light well, which permeates the three levels. The kitchen, living and dining are still on the ground level (although the configuration was changed). On the second level is the main bedroom and what was once a bedroom has been converted into a library/retreat. Lined with bookshelves, the library doubles as a television area. And on the third level are the office (previously a bedroom) and guest bedroom.

The new office is open to the light well. The windows were also enlarged and are now floor to ceiling. Instead of staring at a blank wall, the owners can enjoy leafy aspects over the neighbourhood, together with the natural light from the light well. A new and more generous

skylight above the light well brings in additional light. 'The extension of the light well to the ground level improved the communication links throughout the house. Messages from the study to the kitchen can be transmitted quite clearly without having to climb the stairs,' says Rizzo.

The office has been simply fitted out. There's a continuous bench along one wall and generous storage area above. There are also full-length cupboards on the opposite wall. 'Storage is crucial in designing offices. You should be able to remove everything from the floor, particularly if you want to clean up before a client arrives,' says interior designer Christopher Hansson. Mobile drawers below the desk allow for additional storage and files.

Office

Bedroom 3

Void

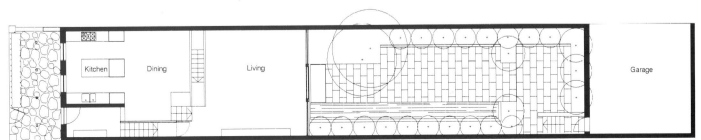

| Kitchen | Dining | Living | | Garage |

THE ENERGY AT LUXE

NEOMETRO ARCHITECTS

Photography by Peter Clarke

NEOMETRO ARCHITECTS WERE LOOKING FOR A NEW SPACE FOR THEIR OFFICE WHEN THEY CAME ACROSS A WAREHOUSE, ON A SITE WITH A MIXED-USE ZONING (RESIDENTIAL AND COMMERCIAL). 'IT WAS A GREAT STARTING POINT. IT MEANT THAT WE COULD DESIGN A BUILDING THAT HAD A TWENTY-FOUR HOUR LIFE CYCLE, WITH PEOPLE COMING AND GOING AT ALL TIMES OF THE DAY, SAYS ARCHITECT CLARE McALLISTER, WHO IS ONE OF THE FOUR DIRECTORS OF THE PRACTICE.

While the original 1950s warehouse was retained, two levels of car parking were created below the building. Two new levels were designed on top of the roof and what was once an open car park on the site was developed into a seven-storey building with links to the existing warehouse. To energise the street as well as the building, a restaurant and bar were designed. And rather than earmark the various units in the building as either office or apartment, the owners and tenants made the decision for themselves. Each space was conceived as a pod, with a service core of kitchen and bathroom and an open plan space. Neometro Architects accommodated three of the units for their office adjacent to a large central terrace. 'We wanted to ensure if anyone built next to us, there was a continual source of light. We were also keen to incorporate a communal garden, where everyone could meet up,' says McAllister. During the warmer months, the large sliding doors to their office can be pulled back and staff can spill out on to the terrace.

The interior of the office has an industrial aesthetic, like the original warehouse on the site. There are polished concrete floors at reception and polished timber in the open plan work areas. The concrete ceiling has simply been painted and the services hanging from the ceiling are deliberately exposed. Even the plywood partitions that define the workstations have a worn feel. 'It's not a precious environment. It's quite a robust studio and can get quite noisy with eighteen people,' says McAllister. However, Neometro Architects also included two meeting rooms that can be screened off by means of large sliding doors. One of the enclosed spaces is used by the four directors. A long timber bench was built in preference to separate offices or even separate workstations.

Music is a constant in the office as is the light which streams through the space. As McAllister says, 'It's a relaxed environment. People aren't restricted in their movements. And when they're not working, they can meet up with other residents in the building, either in the courtyard or in the restaurant'.

VICTORIAN HOTEL

GRANT AMON ARCHITECTS PTY LTD

Photography by Maurice Grant-Drew

THIS GRAND VICTORIAN HOTEL, BUILT IN THE 1880S, ORIGINALLY SERVICED HOLIDAY-MAKERS. NOW CONSIDERED PART OF AN INNER CITY SUBURB, THE HOTEL WAS REJUVENATED IN THE 1990S. THE GROUND FLOOR WAS TURNED INTO A BAR, A RESTAURANT AND A GALLERY. THE FIRST LEVEL WAS CONVERTED INTO RESIDENTIAL AND COMMERCIAL SPACES AND THE THREE UPPER FLOORS BECAME APARTMENTS.

Architect Grant Amon was involved in the transformation and during that time worked from the hotel's original living room. 'When everything had been completed, I thought I would stay,' says Amon. The office, on the first floor, included all the decorative embellishments of the period: an open fireplace, decorative mouldings and cornices, together with Baltic pine flooring (now polished). The space is generous, as are the ceilings, approximately 4 metres in height.

Originally there was a small kitchenette tucked away and what was probably a maid's room adjacent to the living room. Amon turned the maid's room into a second office and converted the kitchenette into a small conference area. A new kitchen, with stainless steel finishes, was then incorporated into the larger office space. 'We had to create a new doorway into the second office. Previously it was only accessible via the main corridor,' says Amon, who also fitted the new office with floor-to-ceiling bookshelves. The open plan office is dotted with benches and a small conference table, tucked into the curved nook of the office, for more informal meetings. Clients requiring more privacy are steered towards the conference area or alternatively towards the generous balconies, which are accessed from all rooms.

The sea views are framed with the building's wrought-iron balustrades and cast-iron columns. While the space is reasonably compact for five people (four working from the larger space and one from the smaller office), the generous dimensions of the spaces and large double-hung windows create a larger picture. As Amon says, 'The sunsets from here are memorable. And we're just above the street. So there's always activity'.

FROM THE INSIDE OUT

HARMER ARCHITECTURE PTY LTD

Photography by Trevor Mein

THIS INNER-CITY OFFICE WAS DESIGNED TO SHOWCASE THE WORK OF HARMER ARCHITECTURE. 'AS AN ARCHITECT YOU SHOULD PRACTICE WHAT YOU PREACH. THIS WAS AN OPPORTUNITY TO DO EXACTLY THAT,' SAYS ARCHITECT PHILIP HARMER.

While the site isn't large, 260 square metres, it was sufficient to provide a new office to cater for up to twenty staff. There was also enough space to include a separate tenancy on an upper level. 'Our previous office was simply too small. We required three times the space,' says Harmer.

The new office is made of concrete panels, concrete suspended floor slabs and a steel-framed roof and has views over the neighbourhood and towards the hills in the distance. Essentially the space was divided into a large open plan area with bench tables. The only enclosed spaces are the conference and meeting rooms. 'We started by designing what we needed on the inside. This determined the design of the exterior,' says Harmer.

The large open work area includes high ceilings (approximately 4 metres) and features aluminium louvres below the ceiling. Natural ventilation was crucial in the space as well as natural light. Hot water coils in the concrete floor slab ensure warmth during the colder months.

The sense that this is no ordinary office starts from the front door. Made of large timber planks inserted with coloured glass, there's a constantly changing play of light on the internal concrete wall leading to the office. The materials used by Harmer for the finishes of the interior delight the senses. The bathroom cubicle, for example, is framed in orange vinyl and nylon netting is used as the balustrade between the ground and first

level. These textures not only provide a contrast to the harder materials such as steel and concrete, but also show potential clients the possibility of using different materials. As Harmer says, 'This place isn't slick. It's meant to look like a workshop. It's a place where we can make models. And more importantly, it's about having a pleasurable space to work in'.

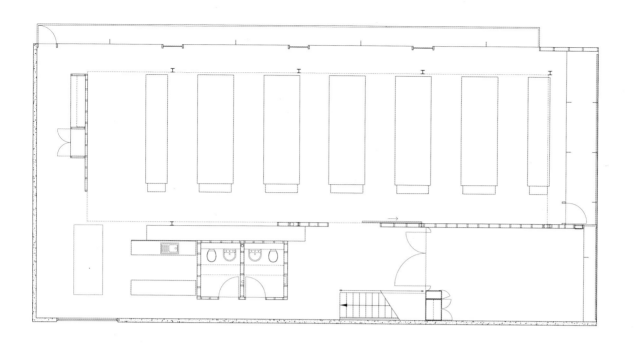

DARE TO BE DIFFERENT

SIX DEGREES

Photography by Rob Blackburn

THIS OFFICE WAS DESIGNED FOR AN ADVERTISING COMPANY CALLED DARE. AND LIKE ITS NAME, THE DESIGN OF THE OFFICE BREAKS NEW GROUND. 'THEY WANTED TO PROVIDE A CONCEPT STORE AND A CAFÉ AS WELL AS AN OFFICE FOR THEIR STAFF,' SAYS ARCHITECT SIMON O'BRIEN, A DIRECTOR OF SIX DEGREES. 'THEY WANTED TO PUT THEMSELVES ON DISPLAY AS WELL AS INVOLVING THE PUBLIC,' ADDS O'BRIEN.

The premises, a stone's throw from the beach, was previously a warehouse and office that had been built in the 1980s. The ground floor was essentially a large car park with a double-height warehouse at the rear. And upstairs were offices, mainly enclosed. While most of the building was gutted for the new venture, the architects retained the two roller doors that lead to the pavement. The architects then extended the ground floor space by adding a timber platform for outdoor eating. They also added large rusted steel columns to the façade. 'They came from a demolition yard. They're quite rough in texture and provide a contrast to the more slick interior,' says O'Brien.

The ground floor exhibits a variety of objects, many of which were found by staff on overseas travels. 'Anything that is of interest, such as a souvenir, becomes an important part of the display,' says O'Brien. The café on the ground floor is used by Dare, as well as the public, with bistro style tables doubling as places for informal meetings.

The Dare offices on the first floor are also one out of the box. The workstations are made of steel and framed with pin-board in a variety of colours. Coloured Perspex, in several hues, further delineates the spaces. 'The workstations can be moved around. They're quite light and can be easily reconfigured,' says O'Brien. The architects also included a raised platform in the design, as an alternative to the more formal boardroom. The long bench style table proudly displays twelve skittles at one end. 'The timber for this table came from a lane in a bowling alley. The skittles couldn't be more appropriate,' he adds. The raised platform also provides views of the beach and the sea. 'It's quite a unique sight,' says O'Brien. The same could be said of the office.

THE RIGHT SERVICE

MULTIPLICITY

Photography by Shania Shegedyn

WHEN TWO REGIONAL COUNCILS AMALGAMATED, THE DECISION
WAS MADE TO ADD A COUPLE OF TEMPORARY HUTS TO AN
EXISTING 1960S COUNCIL BUILDING. THE COST, ALONG WITH
THE EXPEDIENCY OF FOLLOWING THIS PATH SEEMED THE MOST
ATTRACTIVE SOLUTION. HOWEVER ARCHITECT TIM O'SULLIVAN
AND INTERIOR DESIGNER SIOUX CLARK, THE DIRECTORS OF
MULTIPLICITY, PROVIDED A MORE INVENTIVE SCHEME FOR THE
SAME EXPENDITURE.

'They were thinking of simply adding a veranda to the huts to give them a more permanent feel,' says architect Tim O'Sullivan. 'We knew we could come up with a better solution,' he adds.

While their clients were expecting something more substantial than two makeshift huts, they weren't quite prepared for Multiplicity's striking new design. Made of Ecoply and framed by timber poles, the design has a heroic presence. The building is punctuated with deep and slim horizontal windows to frame the views of the shire and to create protection from the harsher sunlight. While the timber poles provide a presence to the street, they also reflect the area's reliance on timber. 'The shire has a strong forestry industry. We thought it was an appropriate response,' says Clark.

The timber colonnade not only creates a striking façade, but combined with corrugated fibreglass, provides a subtle screen to the car park. As the site has a 20 per cent gradient, Multiplicity designed the building to touch the ground only at one point. Raised on stumps, where the land falls away, the building appears considerably lighter than the original red brick offices it is attached to. 'If there's a decision at a later time to develop the site more extensively, this office can simply be put on the back of a truck and moved to another site. It's been designed in modules. So it's not difficult to relocate,' says O'Sullivan.

Inside the new offices, there's a reception area and a small meeting room. And to the rear, are two new enclosed offices, together with a large open plan office area, catering for up to twenty staff. A simple shelving system, made of MDF, simply defines the spaces and provides valuable storage. 'It was important that people working in the original offices don't have to walk through their colleagues' workspaces while they're dealing with clients at the front counter,' says O'Sullivan.

While the new shire offices can be moved to another site, the chances of this occurring are unlikely. The new offices have not only provided valuable space, but importantly, a focus for the region.

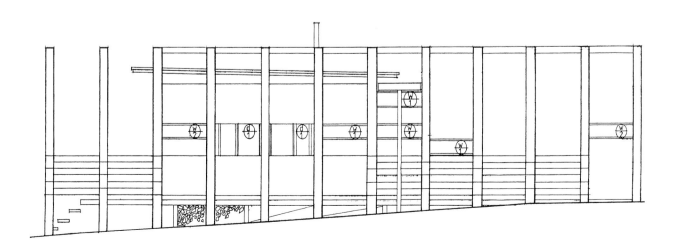

THE RIGHT IMAGINATION

ANNE CRAMPTON ARCHITECT

Photography by David Crampton

IMAGINATION CAN TRANSFORM A PLAIN HOUSE. BUT EVEN THE MOST CREATIVE OF MINDS WOULD HAVE HAD DIFFICULTY WITH THIS ONE WHEN IT CAME ONTO THE MARKET. THE BROWN BRICK FAÇADE WAS PUNCTUATED WITH FLIMSY ALUMINIUM WINDOWS AND THE STAIRCASE TO THE FRONT HEADED IN A NUMBER OF DIRECTIONS. 'WE WANTED TO MOVE INTO SOMETHING MORE CONTEMPORARY THAT WOULD ALLOW US TO CREATE A HOME OFFICE,' SAYS ARCHITECT ANNE CRAMPTON, WHO SHARES THE HOUSE WITH HER HUSBAND, A GRAPHIC DESIGNER AND THEIR TWO CHILDREN.

David and Anne collaborated on the design process, which extended over a twelve-month period. The couple decided to redesign the entire façade. The small, frail aluminium windows were replaced by full-length glass sliding window/walls. And the front balcony was completely removed. The side garden at the front of the house was transformed into the new office wing. The office was designed with an attached conference area, which doubles as a more formal living area. During the day, when the children are at school, the office is available to see clients.

The different levels define the two functions, with the office and conference area on the lower level and the home a few steps above. 'There's a clean point of entry by means of the 'floating' steel stairs to the front entrance, which mark the office and home entrance. While clients can tour the house for ideas for their own home, in most cases, they walk directly into the office area.

Even though the office is not large, it's deceptively spacious as a result of full-length glass windows with views through to the garden. The simple built-in desk along one wall, complete with overhead bookshelves, creates a streamlined effect. The same streamlined approach was taken in the conference area, with a bank of timber cupboards concealing the domestic functions of the house (such as the television set). While the main kitchen and living area is clearly visible from the conference area, the change in level clearly denotes the changes in function.

This home office might have once been considered the least desirable property in the street. It's now an inviting place for both family and clients. The project is also a fine example of what's possible with both imagination and talent.

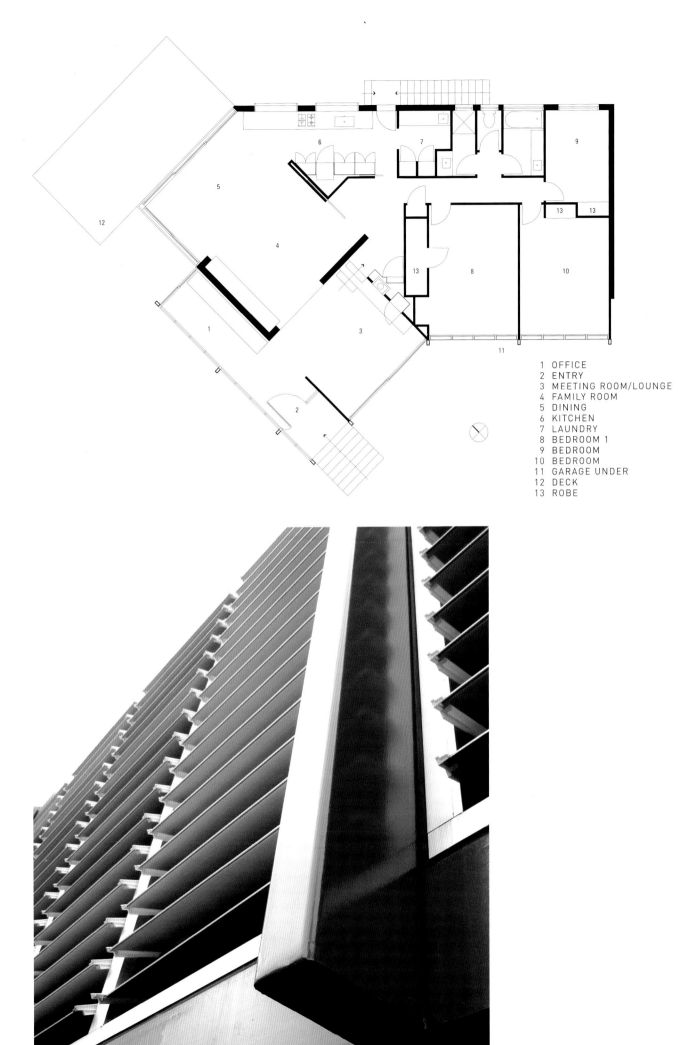

1 OFFICE
2 ENTRY
3 MEETING ROOM/LOUNGE
4 FAMILY ROOM
5 DINING
6 KITCHEN
7 LAUNDRY
8 BEDROOM 1
9 BEDROOM
10 BEDROOM
11 GARAGE UNDER
12 DECK
13 ROBE

CENTRE OF TOWN

STANIC HARDING ARCHITECTS

Photography by Paul Gosney

LOCATED IN THE CENTRE OF TOWN, THIS SIXTEEN-STOREY OFFICE TOWER FEATURES TWO STRIKING PENTHOUSE APARTMENTS THAT ARE BOTH SPREAD OVER TWO LEVELS. HOWEVER, UNLIKE MOST PENTHOUSES, THE GROUND FLOOR OF EACH APARTMENT FEATURES A LUXURIOUS OFFICE. 'THE BRIEF WAS TO CREATE A HIGH QUALITY OFFICE SPACE. OUR CLIENTS ALSO WANTED A "CRASH PAD", SOMEWHERE TO STAY IF WORKING LATE, OR SIMPLY A PLACE FOR INTERSTATE AND OVERSEAS GUESTS TO STAY WHILE IN TOWN,' SAYS ARCHITECT ANDY HARDING OF STANIC HARDING ARCHITECTS.

The office on the lower level (level 15) includes a reception area, tucked into a nook beside the front door, and a waiting area. Behind two massive doors is a large open plan office, with an informal lounge area. A desk is positioned adjacent to soaring glass windows and within the double-height void, measuring approximately 6 metres, to the second level. Limestone flooring in the office creates a luxurious finish, as do gold mosaic tiles that line the walls of the kitchenette and bathroom facilities. Concealed behind two doors that look like wall panels is the entry to the apartment above, while the other leads to the kitchenette. 'It was intentionally designed as a jewellery box. People waiting to go into the office don't know what's there unless they ask to use the bathroom,' says Harding.

Upstairs is an open plan apartment. There's a galley-style kitchen, a meals area, a lounge area and a large bedroom with ensuite facilities. And while the two levels are visually linked, they are separated on the upper level by means of a joinery unit that holds the television and stereo units. 'You can look into the office from above. But it's reasonably private,' says Harding, who acknowledges that clients are fairly taken with the office space, particularly for the first time. Also impressive is the way the cars are parked below the tower. There are no ramps and cars are simply 'stacked' above each other by means of a conveyor belt system. As Harding says, 'It's quite a special office. It's understandable that many guests want to extend their stay'.

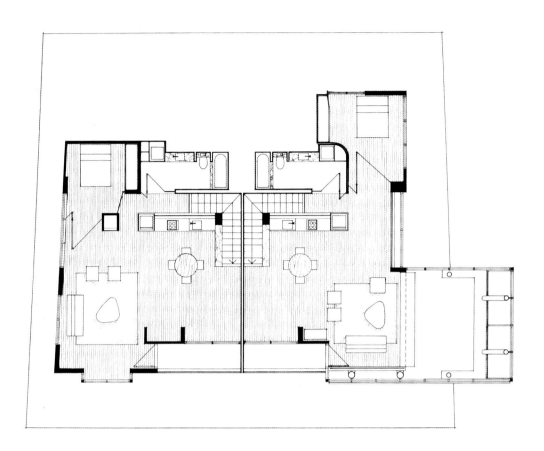

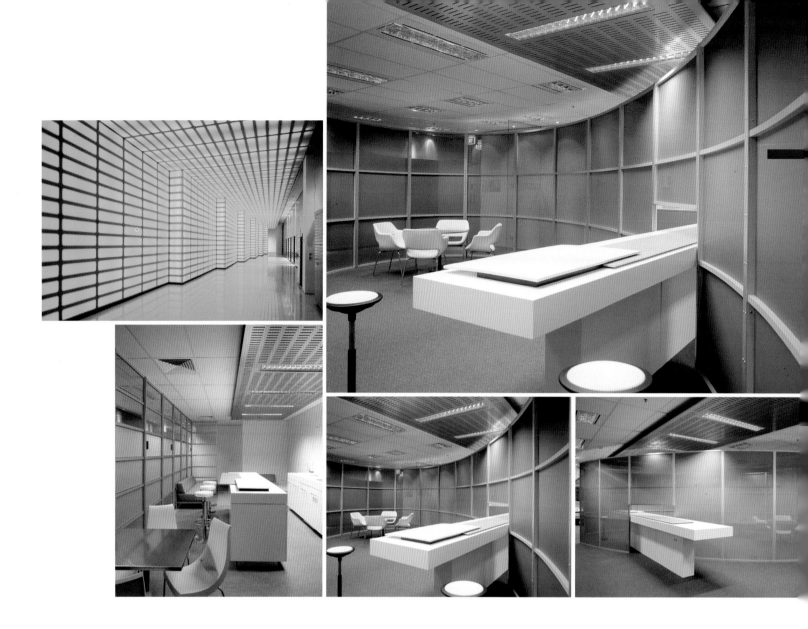

OVER THIRTEEN FLOORS

PECKVONHARTEL

Photography by Dan Magree

DESIGNED IN 1971 BY ARCHITECTS YUNCKEN FREEMAN, THIS INNER-CITY OFFICE TOWER REMAINED EMPTY FOR SEVERAL YEARS. CONSIDERED DATED BY POTENTIAL TENANTS, THE OFFICE IS NOW ONE OF THE MOST IMPRESSIVE ON THE BLOCK. 'IN DESIGN CIRCLES IT WAS ALWAYS CONSIDERED AN EXCEPTIONAL BUILDING,' SAYS ARCHITECT YVONNE VON HARTEL, A DIRECTOR OF PECKVONHARTEL.

One of the reasons there was little interest recently was because of the main foyer to the building. Known as 'Eagle Star' (after an English insurance company), the foyer was dissected by a large wall with the Eagle emblem. To entice developers, the architects constructed a lime green resin wall, backlit with fluorescent lighting. Even before it was constructed, the architects presented the developers with a CAD animation of the design. 'It sold the scheme and they couldn't wait to see what we had in mind for the whole building,' says von Hartel.

Fourteen floors in the building are now occupied by the Deloitte Consulting Group. And while the interior is now sharp and contemporary, the architects were fortunate to inherit exceptional floor plates. 'With most office buildings, there a

central lift core and the spaces are organised around it. In this case, the lifts and services were already on the perimeter,' says von Hartel. 'It allowed for a more efficient design,' she adds.

Elliptical breakout spaces were inserted in the core areas of each floor. Made of resin and aluminium, these 'cages' create a continuous flow of light throughout the office. These spaces also double as informal meeting areas, with kitchenettes attached. 'The spaces have to be extremely flexible. Some staff work full time, others require 'hot-desking'. Some of the consultants might only need to come into the office for a few hours a day,' says von Hartel. With this in mind, many of the offices on the perimeter can be used as single offices or combined for meetings.

In contrast to the curvaceous breakout areas, there's a strong linearity in the design. A polished aluminium panel hovers just below the ceiling and conceals many of the services in the offices. The vibrant green used in the building's foyer was also introduced into the interiors, making an appearance in lounges and in workstations. As von Hartel says, 'Most offices tend to go for grey. This green is evocative of the green glass used in the original building (façade). There's also a connection to the outdoors'.

SUBSTANCE

HASSELL

Photography by Earl Carter

THE WORD 'SUBSTANCE' WAS USED IN THE BRIEF FOR THIS
CORPORATE DESIGN. AND THERE'S CERTAINLY SUBSTANCE TO
THIS FIT-OUT FOR THE LAW FIRM ALLENS ARTHUR ROBINSON,
WHICH HAS OFFICES ALL OVER THE WORLD.

Designed by Hassell, clients are greeted with a timber-lined foyer and stained oak panelling that extends to the ceiling. Reminiscent of a comfortable lounge, there's an instant sense of warmth. Horizontal timber panelling leads the eye directly to the reception counter, constructed in stone.

While all the previous design elements were removed, Hassell retained a sweeping curved staircase that links two floors. The designers added bronze metal to frame the spandrel between the two levels of the office. 'The reflective panelling diffuses the mass of the spandrel and adds a reflective quality between the floors,' says interior designer Robert Backhouse.

Hassell treated the spaces as three distinct zones. Firstly, there are the core areas, delineated by dark timber walls. These areas include small meeting rooms, service areas such as the kitchen and the client business centre. A second zone is called the transition zone, which separates the inner core from spaces on the perimeter. Used as a gallery to display part of the firm's art collection, the transition space has a 'lowered' ceiling. And the third zone, on the perimeter, features a distinctive aluminium battened ceiling. 'The materials become lighter as you're drawn towards the natural light at the perimeter'.

Hassell designed a variety of configurations for clients to meet with staff. Lounge areas, similar to those found in a hotel, occupy two corners of

the floor plate. Complete with comfortable lounge suites, marble-topped bars, silk raffia wallpaper and artwork, there's a sense of familiarity as well as formality. 'It's an alternative way of meeting clients. The lounge areas might be used to sign contracts. Alternatively, they can be used to conduct interviews,' says Backhouse, who points out the large injected resin glass sliding walls that divide many of the spaces. As Backhouse adds, 'They create privacy, but still allow a degree of transparency between the spaces'.

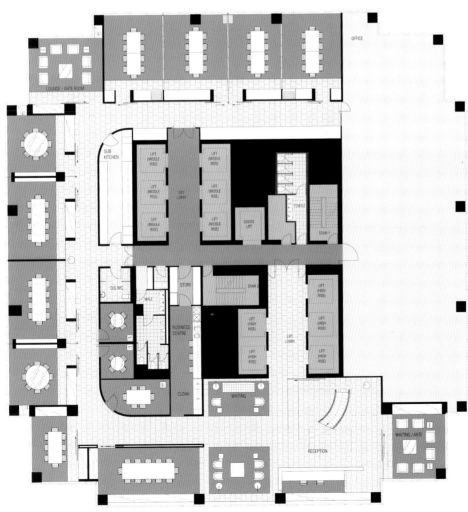

A COMPLETE MAKEOVER

HASSELL

Photography by Trevor Mein

NOTHING REMAINS OF THE PREVIOUS FIT-OUT ON LEVELS 20 AND 21 OF THIS CITY OFFICE BUILDING. 'IT WAS A COMPLETE MAKEOVER. WE DID IT IN FIVE STAGES,' SAYS INTERIOR DESIGNER ROBERT BACKHOUSE OF HASSELL. DESIGNED FOR THE REAL ESTATE COMPANY JONES LANG LASALLE, THE MAKEOVER REFLECTS A CHANGE IN BUSINESS STYLE. 'THE WAY WE DO BUSINESS HAS CHANGED. IT'S NOT JUST A SPACE FOR PEOPLE TO WORK IN, BUT A PLACE WHERE PEOPLE INTERACT'.

People arrive and find themselves standing in a stainless box (lift core), before moving towards a reception area that is slightly elevated, along with two adjacent offices, one which is used as a boardroom. Hassell wanted to create the sense of a pavilion, a 'building within a building'. As a result, the shadow lines on the floor and ceiling create a 'floating structure'. Opposite the reception area is an open meeting area. All these areas are framed by bronze tinted glass, creating privacy for the users. 'People walking down the corridors can only see the outline of people. And for those using these spaces, there's still the unimpeded views of the city,' says Backhouse.

The lounge area can be used to meet both clients and as a waiting area for clients. However, people tend to sit on the bench style seating near reception. 'The lounge area is there to be used. It really activates the space,' says Backhouse, who explains the contrast between the enclosed glass pavilions and the mostly open plan areas over the two levels of the office. 'Our clients are continually working in teams. There might be two staff working together, or as many as eighteen. The workstations are deliberately designed to be lightweight. The stations are continually moved around'.

On the lower level are more workstations, together with a central bar and kitchen. The architects were conscious of integrating the two levels and were keen to ensure there was maximum movement among staff. 'We deliberately placed the staircase near the kitchen. We didn't want staff to feel it was two companies working in the same building,' says Backhouse. The bar, referred to as the Hub, includes tables and chairs, a bar and a plasma screen. As Backhouse says, 'It's not just about work. It might be used for informal gatherings or even a cocktail party'.

A VICTORIAN SHOPFRONT

DAVID NEIL ARCHITECTS

Photography by Shannon McGrath

THIS VICTORIAN STYLE SHOP STILL RETAINS ITS HANDSOME FAÇADE. BUT WHAT WAS ONCE A RETAIL ENVIRONMENT IS NOW AN OFFICE FOR ARCHITECT DAVID NEIL. 'WE COMPLETELY GUTTED THE GROUND FLOOR (THE FIRST FLOOR IS USED AS A RESIDENCE). IT WAS ESSENTIALLY CARVED INTO SEVERAL SMALLER ROOMS,' SAYS ARCHITECT DAVID NEIL. 'THERE WAS NO KITCHEN AND THE BATHROOM COULD ONLY BE ACCESSED FROM THE OUTSIDE,' HE ADDS.

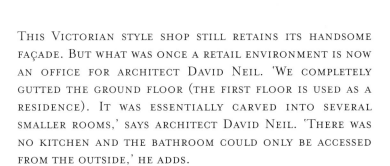

While the configuration of space was not ideal, the position opposite a large suburban park was a major drawcard. The large shop front window offered a scenic view. Neil removed the partitions and made the ground floor one long space, defined by changing levels (two in total) and original nibbed walls. At the rear of the space, the width narrows to only 2.8 metres. So the nibbed walls now act as alcoves for the desks, which were designed in one continuous line over two levels.

Made of American oak, a freestanding unit conceals the fax machine, printer and provides storage for paper. And in the centre of the unit, Neil designed a layout bench, for extra workspace, or for looking at reference material. Floor-to-ceiling bookshelves complete the library. 'We were conscious of keeping the office fairly streamlined. We were happy for clients to see the workings of the office. But the view should be orderly,' says Neil.

While the views through the shop front are idyllic, the views to the side lane simply highlighted a brick wall. To camouflage the view, the architects installed a large translucent glass panel across the window, allowing morning light to still enter the space.

Although the main view over the park is best appreciated from the meeting area at the front of the house, staff can also enjoy the outlook from their desks. Elevated and without the interference of partitions, there's an unimpeded view.

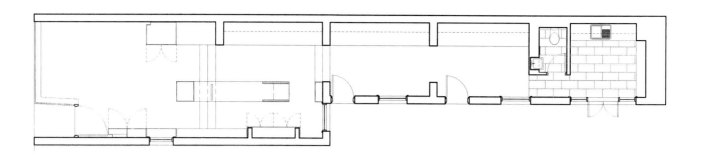

NEW LIFE FOR AN EIGHTIES BUILDING

SJB ARCHITECTS

Photography by Tony Miller

THIS BUILDING DIDN'T DIFFERENTIATE ITSELF FROM ITS NEIGHBOURS. BUILT IN THE 1980S, IT SHARED THE SAME SMALL STRIP WINDOWS FOUND ON THE STRIP. HOWEVER, ITS POSITION ON A MAIN ROAD ON THE EDGE OF THE CITY WAS SUFFICIENT FOR PROBUILD CONSTRUCTIONS TO CONSIDER THIS PROPERTY FOR ITS HEADQUARTERS.

SJB Architects designed this three-storey building in the 1980s. Twenty years later, they were asked by Probuild, who they regularly work with, to come up with a new design, one that would create a stronger gesture to the street. What was once a three-storey walk-up arrangement is now an impressive office, complete with obligatory lift. 'We essentially gutted the entire building. The only thing retained was the floor slabs and the structure. We also added to the floor space by increasing the footprint on the third level,' says architect Alfred de Bryne.

While the original workstations were larger, they were considerably less efficient. There are different storage strategies now, and different computer equipment. 'There are a variety of expectations that have to be met,' says de Bryne. The three floors, which include meeting rooms, workstations, enclosed offices and staff amenities, are completely different from their previous configurations.

The most dramatic change to the building appears in the façade and the reception area at street level. Horizontal windows were replaced by a two-storey glazed façade, angled beyond the building's alignment. And the reception area, which extends nearly the full width of the ground floor, acts as a showcase for the company's work. The reception area includes a striking stone feature wall, together with a graphic staircase to one side. Even the furniture in the reception area is low to the floor to allow for an unimpeded view into the building.

As de Bryne says, 'Our clients wanted a strong and confident statement. They wanted their headquarters to have a presence to the street. And there had to be a generosity of scale'.

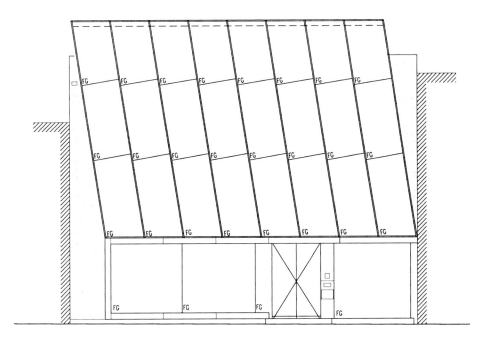

DESIGNED FOR A LIFETIME

WHITTAKER HADENHAM OPENSHAW PTY LTD

Photography by Marcus Clinton

THE ARCHITECTS OF THIS PROJECT WERE INTRODUCED TO THEIR CLIENTS, REAL ESTATE AGENCY BICKMORE HUTT, VIA A BRAND IMAGE AND MANAGEMENT CONSULTANT, KNOWN AS GORILLA. 'THEY WANTED TO POSITION THEMSELVES IN A COMPLETELY DIFFERENT WAY TO THEIR COMPETITORS,' SAYS GRAEME HADENHAM, A DIRECTOR OF WHITTAKER HADENHAM OPENSHAW (WHO). 'THEY REGARD THEMSELVES AS "THE AGENCY FOR LIFE", WHERE RELATIONSHIPS DEVELOP OVER A LIFETIME,' SAYS HADENHAM.

The first noticeable difference is the position the agency occupies in the three-storey building. It's a first-floor office with minimal street exposure. The only sign of the office from the street is a glimpse of the large graphic backdrop behind the reception desk. 'The idea was to create a sense of going into a client's home. It seemed appropriate since a significant part of their business is carried out in clients' homes after hours,' says Hadenham.

As in a home, there's a pond on arrival, with a ledge that doubles as a waiting area. However, clients generally choose to wait or discuss their business informally in the lounge area, complete with armchairs. WHO also included an open plan kitchen and bar area adjacent to the lounge area, in order to create a variety of meeting arrangements.

Two simple partition walls create the divisions. Behind the lounge area is an open plan meeting area with a central table. And behind another partition is another informal meeting area, consisting of a few armchairs and a coffee table. The remainder of the office (with the exception of bathrooms) is completely open. The workstations, designed on the perimeter of the space, are open to the workings of the office. 'They wanted to have a completely open arrangement. They wanted to have a sense of transparency. It's the way they do business,' says Hadenham.

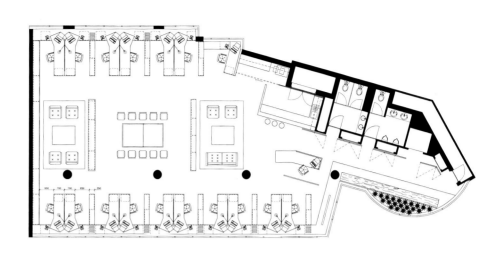

A SENSE OF THE PAST

WHITTAKER HADENHAM OPENSHAW PTY LTD
Photography by Marcus Clinton

DESIGNED BY WHITTAKER HADENHAM OPENSHAW (WHO) FOR THE ADVERTISING COMPANY D'ARCY, THIS OFFICE, ON THE FRINGE OF THE CITY EXTENDS OVER 1000 SQUARE METRES ON ONE LEVEL. PREVIOUSLY, THE SPACE FEATURED A 1980S FIT-OUT, COMPLETE WITH MUSHROOM PAINTED WALLS AND EXTENSIVE PARTITIONS. 'WE GUTTED THE ENTIRE LEVEL AND REMOVED ANY TRACE OF THE EIGHTIES,' SAYS ARCHITECT GRAEME HADENHAM, A DIRECTOR OF THE PRACTICE.

The clients were keen to create an interior that reflected their organisation. 'They wanted a space that had character, but they were also keen to reflect the past. They had a genuine interest in heritage buildings,' says Hadenham. 'They were keen to include a raw industrial aesthetic,' he adds. Recycled railway sleepers were incorporated in the design and used as walls to define spaces.

Clients first see a pond upon arrival, together with a raised timber deck area that resembles a patio. The patio, framed with original glass-louvred windows, allows for informal meetings. 'This area used to be a veranda. We accentuated

the sense of outdoors by using timber on the floor and including outdoor style furniture,' says Hadenham, who adds it's now one of the most popular places for both staff and clients to meet. 'They do their pitches there. It just has that relaxed quality about it,' he adds. However, there are alternative open plinth-like arrangements in the space, should the veranda not be available.

For more formal presentations, there are two glazed pavilion-like rooms in the centre of the office. While the rooms are transparent, their glass walls allow for some privacy. Both of these pavilions have fold-back doors at either end that

allow for a more open configuration if required. 'They're similar to a glass pod. They're slightly elevated to create a floating effect,' says Hadenham. For the most part, the offices are open plan, with workstations arranged either side of pavilion-like offices. The only division between stations are shelving units. 'The design allows for groups of people to work together. It's about spontaneous communication and sharing ideas'.

Staff and clients appreciate the relaxed and informal lounge and kitchen areas in the office. Complete with bar stools and timber tables, there's a sense of being at home.

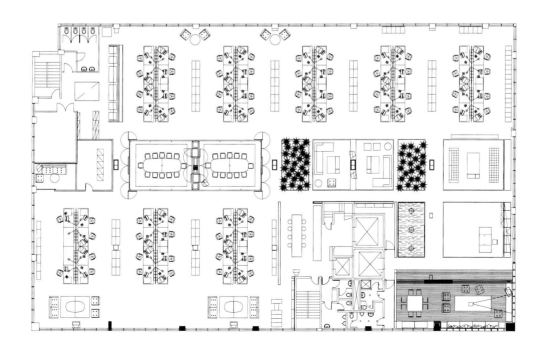

OVER SIX LEVELS

WHITTAKER HADENHAM OPENSHAW PTY LTD

Photography by Marcus Clinton

DESIGNED OVER SIX LEVELS FOR ADVERTISING COMPANY GEORGE PATTERSON BATES, THIS OFFICE HAS APPROXIMATELY 5000 SQUARE METRES OF SPACE. WITH WHITE POLISHED FLOORS AND OPEN PLAN SPACES, THE SIZE OF THIS OFFICE APPEARS CONSIDERABLY GREATER.

Designed by Whittaker Hadenham Openshaw (WHO), bow-shaped floor plates over the six levels provide a strong connection. The architects incorporated a dramatic steel and glass stair to link the various floors. Using a LED lighting system, the entire colour spectrum appears at different times of the day. 'It's like a glass sculpture. It also works like a light well,' says architect Graeme Hadenham.

The brief from the clients was to create a space that had a sense of energy. They wanted a hard edge to the interior. 'That's how the white glossy finish came about,' says Hadenham. While the entire office is linked by the staircase, it was important to provide each level with separate facilities, such as a café on every floor. Located adjacent to the stairwell, staff can easily mingle with colleagues on a lower or higher level. There are also a couple of enclosed meeting areas clustered around the café areas.

As the lift core occupies a central position in the building (a feature inherited by the architects), the open plan work areas on either side of the core are relatively narrow (approximately 7 metres in width). In response to this constraint, WHO designed steel and glass desks in spans of 7 metres. The desk system, which appears to cantilever above the space, was designed in collaboration with the Italian company Unifor. In addition to bench style workstations, staff can use the window ledges for seating. Unlike many other offices, there's also no hierarchical arrangement. Everyone works from a central bench, even the CEO. 'Our clients were quite excited about this arrangement. They came from offices, where every space was enclosed with partitions'.

There's no formal reception area. Instead, there's a small concierge desk near the entrance. The concierge simply walks down the corridor to meet clients. As Hadenham says, 'It's quite informal. You feel as though you're arriving at someone's home'.

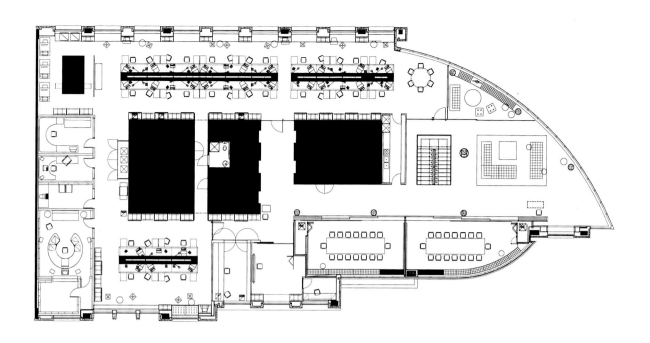

INSPIRATIONAL

DI DONATO

Photography by Earl Carter

THIS OFFICE HAS GIVEN DI DONATO, A DESIGN MANAGEMENT
COMPANY, A STRONG PRESENCE IN AN INNER CITY STREET.
BUILT IN THE LATE 1980S BY ARCHITECTS COUCH AND CARTER,
THE THREE-STOREY CONCRETE AND STEEL OFFICE BUILDING
HAS THE MORE SLEEK AND INDUSTRIAL FEEL OF THE LATE 90S.

Tony Di Donato, the director of the practice, recalls the first time he entered the building. 'It was the sheer volume of the three-storey light well that probably took us in first. It was also the very raw finishes that were used, concrete walls, exposed steel beams and that "cage". The cage was almost primitive in feel,' he adds. The cage to which Di Donato refers is a product of the grid-like walls that separate the spaces from the void.

Only minor work was required by Di Donato. 'One of the main changes carried out was the lighting. The work that we're involved in requires precise lighting. Even though the natural light was terrific during the day, the more ambient lighting for the evenings wasn't right,' he says. The central staircase that encroached on valuable floor space was removed. A spiral staircase, in vibrant yellow, was subsequently installed and now acts as the core of the office. 'It's a bit like a spear that pierces through each level,' says Di Donato.

The reception desk and workstation were designed by Ism Objects for Di Donato's previous office, a Victorian terrace. 'We knew that our next move would be something that was modern and we wanted something that we could take with us.'

The apartment on the top level of this building remains in its original condition and typifies the building's strong industrial origins. Raw steel beams meet with an exposed aluminium insulated ceiling, which is only partly concealed by a fine mesh screen. As Di Donato says, 'This building is really an inherent part of the business. The staff are continually stimulated by their surrounds and can therefore produce highly creative work'.

RESPONDING TO THE SITE

LYONS

Photography by John Gollings, Trevor Mein, Martin Saunders

THIS NEW BUILDING WAS DESIGNED BY LYONS, FOR THE SCHOOL OF BOTANY AT THE UNIVERSITY OF MELBOURNE. ABUTTING AN ALLEY, KNOWN AS TIN ALLEY, THE TWO-STOREY BUILDING ALSO OVERLOOKS A SIGNIFICANT GARDEN, INCLUDING A MORETON BAY FIG TREE. 'THE UNIVERSITY WANTED TO CREATE MORE OF A STREET FRONTAGE FOR THE SCHOOL. THEY HAVE STRONG LINKS TO INDUSTRY AND WERE KEEN TO HAVE A MORE FRONT DOOR ADDRESS,' SAYS ARCHITECT CLARE CONNAN OF LYONS.

To simulate an urban environment, Lyons used robust materials. The façade to the alley consists of glazed bricks, Alucobond (aluminium) and glass for the windows. The aluminium was designed in a series of folds, allowing the windows to be shaded and removing the need for an obtrusive canopy. In contrast to the more public façade, the other side of the building, overlooking the garden, is more reflective. Lyons used a series of coloured glass panels to capture the immediate environment. Red, brown and orange glass appears at the lowest rung of the building, before changing to greens on the middle rung. Blue and purple glass spans across

the highest band. 'The colours reflect the ground, the foliage of the trees and the sky,' says Connan. The glass also acts as a mirror, creating reflections of the landscape.

Inside the building, there are several enclosed offices as well as a large meeting area/conference room. 'It's a large multipurpose function area (referring to the conference area). It can be used for lectures or alternatively can be closed off to form smaller spaces,' says Connan. As there are a number of different departments within the school, many of the offices had to be enclosed. However, unlike many offices, where

ceiling heights are low, they are generous, up to 3.4 metres in height. Windows, both high and low, allow air to circulate during the day, with the higher windows providing night cooling at the end of the day.

The System garden, which plays an integral role in the project, was established by the University of Melbourne in 1856. Mindful of its importance, Lyons was keen not only to fully integrate the garden into the design, but also to create a building that would reflect its significance.

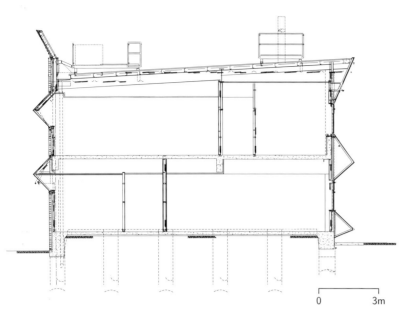

0   3m

TWO IN ONE

SHELTON FINNIS PTY LTD

Photography by Lynton Crabb

THIS OFFICE FIT-OUT, BY SHELTON FINNIS ARCHITECTS, WAS DESIGNED FOR TWO COMPANIES. HOWEVER, INSTEAD OF CREATING TWO COMPLETELY DISTINCT OFFICES, THE BOUNDARIES ARE BLURRED. BOTH STAFF AND CLIENTS ACCESS THE BUILDING VIA A BACK LANE, THEN WALK THROUGH A SERVICE AREA AND UP TWO FLIGHTS OF STAIRS. 'OUR CLIENTS LIKE THE APPROACH. IT'S NOT THE USUAL LIFT TO RECEPTION,' SAYS ARCHITECT SCOTT SHELTON.

The reception area, made of oak and laminate, features a cerise inset panel. To one side is the office of Renegade Films, on the other side is Style Counsel, a fashion-based company. And between the two, directly behind the reception area is an enclosed meeting area, with doors on either side. 'This area is shared by both companies. It's just a matter of making sure the space is free,' says Shelton.

The office of Renegade Films consists of one large open plan space, a seating area, a kitchenette, an editing room, together with the shared meeting space. Long timber benches, approximately 6 metres in length, are used for both staff and client meetings, as well as for everyday work. The office of Style Counsel is slightly more traditional in layout, with a number of enclosed offices as well as open plan areas.

While the building, a 1920s warehouse, had to be completely gutted by the architects, the space did possess some appealing original features, such as large floor-to-ceiling curved windows down one side of the building and original timber floors. 'It feels like a typical New York loft space. The ceiling heights are generous and you don't know what to expect from the street,' says Shelton. And while clients still find it difficult to find the offices, they're delighted when they do. 'Most people (staff and clients) appreciate the open plan arrangement. The internal walls don't reach the ceiling, so the spaces appear continuous. And importantly, the arrangement seems to work,' says Shelton.

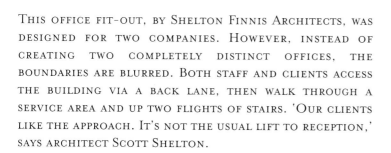

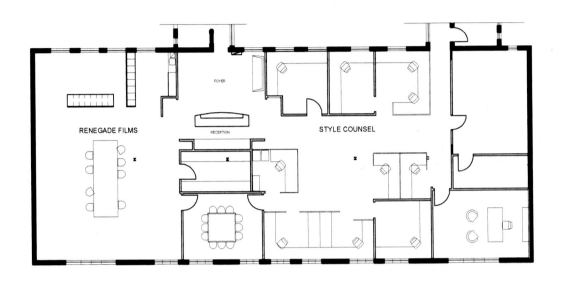

RENEGADE FILMS
FOYER
RECEPTION
STYLE COUNSEL

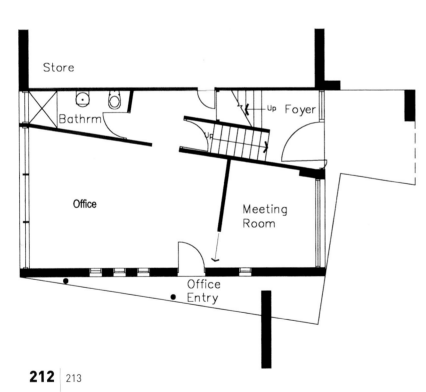

Store

Bathrm

Office

Up Foyer

UP

Meeting
Room

Office
Entry

A LEAFY ENCLAVE

BRUCE MARSHALL ARCHITECTS

Photography by Bruce Marshall

THIS HOME OFFICE IS JUST OVER 5 KILOMETRES FROM THE CITY. IN A LEAFY STREET, IT DOUBLES AS THE HOME AND OFFICE FOR ARCHITECT BRUCE MARSHALL. THE STRIKING CONTEMPORARY BUILDING IS UNRECOGNISABLE FROM THE ORIGINAL HOME ON THE SITE, A 1920S CALIFORNIAN BUNGALOW. MARSHALL REWORKED THE ENTIRE HOUSE AND THE SITE. 'WE EXCAVATED 300 CUBIC METRES OF SOIL,' SAYS MARSHALL, WHO CREATED A NEW LEVEL BELOW GROUND FOR THE OFFICE. THE LIVING, KITCHEN AND DINING AREA ON THE FIRST FLOOR OF THE HOUSE WERE REDESIGNED AND A NEW ENTRANCE PLACED TO THE SIDE. 'IT WAS IMPORTANT TO CREATE COMPLETE SEPARATION FROM THE HOME. THE OFFICE HAD TO HAVE A SENSE OF COMPLETE AUTONOMY,' SAYS MARSHALL.

The architectural practice, which has four staff, wanted to make a statement about the work it are known for and keen to produce. 'The design had to be contemporary and have clean lines. I also wanted to play with light,' says Marshall, who framed the office with a large slot window to the garden and a series of floor to ceiling windows looking towards the street. 'It was important to make a connection with the street. It's a quiet street and people walking past enliven the office,' says Marshall.

The office consists of a U-shaped bench with workstations, together with a central table for looking at plans and discussing ideas. There's also a separate meeting area that contains the printing and photocopying machines. An acidic yellow feature wall with a sliding door creates a partition between the two work areas. As Marshall says, 'The office has quite a tranquil feel. Your eye is drawn to the garden beds rather than the sky. You always feel quite grounded'.

GOING TO WORK

COY & YIONTIS PTY LTD

Photography by Peter Clarke

ONLY THE FRONT TWO ROOMS REMAIN OF THIS HERITAGE-LISTED, INNER-CITY VICTORIAN TERRACE. ON ONE SIDE OF THE ORIGINAL HALLWAY IS A STUDY AND ON THE OTHER SIDE IS A BEDROOM. HOWEVER, PAST THESE TWO ROOMS, THE HOUSE IS ENTIRELY NEW AND UNASHAMEDLY CONTEMPORARY.

Designed by Coy Yiontis Architects, the study at the front of the house forms part of one of three pavilions. The other two pavilions are kitchen, living and dining (also on the ground floor) and the main bedroom and ensuite on the first level. While the study, the front bedroom and bathroom are separated from the main living area by a courtyard and pond, there is a covered walkway to form a bridge. 'The front pavilion is like a gatehouse. The idea is to experience the elements as you pass from one pavilion to the next,' says architect Rosa Coy. 'Our client works from home. It was important that he felt he was leaving the house and going to work,' she says.

The study, which occupies one of the original front rooms, has two entirely different vistas. The front vista to the street features the original window with plantation shutters (for ventilation). The other vista looks backs into the house, through the courtyard and into the main living space. The massive picture window (2.7 metres by 2 metres) creates a sense of space and connects with the elements. 'You can see into the main living space from the study. But there's a sheer blind that can be pulled down in the living room if separation is required,' says Coy.

The study, like the rest of the house, was designed in a minimal style. A workstation along one wall is the main piece of furniture. 'The idea was to keep it simple and create a tranquil environment,' says Coy. And for the owner, there's a clear separation between work and leisure.

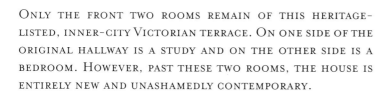

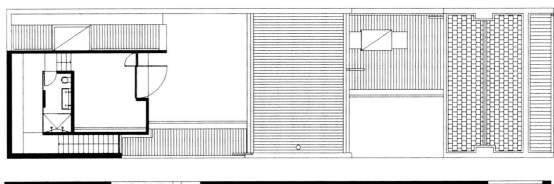

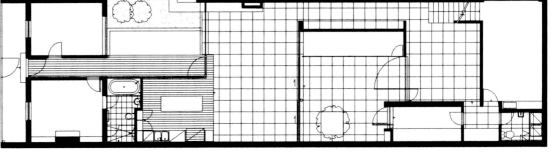

ONE LARGE SPACE

CASSANDRA FAHEY

Photography by Michael Ben-Meir

ARCHITECT CASSANDRA FAHEY'S NEW HOME OFFICE IS ONE
LARGE OPEN SPACE. DIRECTLY BELOW THE APARTMENT WHERE
SHE LIVES WITH HER PARTNER MICHAEL BEN-MEIR, IT'S LESS
THAN 30 SECONDS BEFORE SHE'S IN WORK MODE.

The office occupies the ground level of a factory, built around the turn of the last century. Originally it was used to produce sweets and in more recent times was used by a car mechanic. When Fahey and Ben-Meir bought the building, it was little more than a shell. The only remnants of its former life were the timber trusses on the first floor and the timber ceiling and floor below.

Fortunately, there were two separate entrances to the building, a double set of doors to the office and a separate door to the apartment. There's also a pair of gold timber doors halfway up the staircase. 'There's a clear distinction between the home and the office. You need to be able to close off from things at the end of the day,' says Fahey.

The large open plan office has double doors at one end and a single door at the other. Fahey inserted glass into the original doors that abut the footpath to create an open feel to the street. 'Most people don't even knock. They just walk in straight in,' says Fahey, who deliberately wanted an informal office space. Shelves are open and plans and models are dotted around the office. 'It's not a precious space. There are no divisions and no hierarchy. The only area that's concealed is the kitchenette (behind a screen),' says Fahey. Clients can discuss ideas at the workstations or over coffee in the lounge area.

As Fahey says, 'You'll generally find the communication and interaction between staff is much better when it's on the same level. It's a reasonably small office and you always need to know what's going on'.

SYMMETRICAL

GUILFORD BELL + GRAHAM FISHER ARCHITECTS

Photography by Shannon McGrath

THIS HOME OFFICE, IN THE CENTRE OF A LARGE FAMILY HOME, WAS PART OF A LARGER RENOVATION BY GUILFORD BELL + GRAHAM FISHER ARCHITECTS. THE OFFICE, LOCATED BETWEEN THE PASSAGE TO THE KITCHEN AND THE MAIN LIVING AREA, OCCUPIES ONE OF THE DARKEST AREAS WITHIN THE HOUSE. 'I DIDN'T WANT THE OFFICE TO BE LOCATED IN A COMPLETELY SEPARATE ROOM. THIS "HATCH" IS REALLY CONNECTED TO THE MAIN LIVING SPACES,' SAYS ARCHITECT GRAHAM FISHER.

A spectacular view of the river through large picture windows in the living areas, was a driving force in the design of the office. 'You walk down the passage and through the study to the living area. It's about going from a dark, quite sombre ambience to a much lighter environment,' says Fisher.

The office has white walls and Australian walnut timber shelves, some of which were specifically designed to display books. There's also a built-in walnut timber desk to accommodate both the owners. 'It's a place to work. But it's also about connecting to the living room and displaying photos and objects,' says Fisher, who extended the design by projecting two shelves through the white walls dividing the study from the living area. The open hatches allow communication with the family while they're watching television and the extended shelves are used to support the stereo equipment on one side.

A series of columns frame the study area, creating a rhythm in the design and a sense of symmetry this architectural practice is renowned for. This symmetry is highlighted by the egg shaped light positioned on the newel post at the bottom of the stairs. 'The light creates a central axis in the design. It also illuminates the darkest point in the house,' says Fisher.

While the river in the distance is a feature of this house, the office area is intriguing in itself. People linger and explore the books before moving to the lighter edge.